BUILDING TYPE BASICS FOR

housing

SECOND EDITION

BUILDING TYPE BASICS FOR

housing

SECOND EDITION

ROBERT CHANDLER, JOHN CLANCY, DAVID DIXON,
JOAN GOODY, GEOFFREY WOODING,
Goody Clancy: Architecture, Planning, Preservation

WILEY

JOHN WILEY & SONS, INC.

Copyright © 2010 by John Wiley & Sons, Inc. All rights reserved

Published by John Wiley & Sons, Inc., Hoboken, New Jersey
Published simultaneously in Canada

Interior layout and production: Jeff Baker

Library of Congress Cataloging-in-Publication Data:

Building type basics for housing / Stephen A. Kliment, series founder and editor ; Robert Chandler ...
[et al.] ; Goody Clancy, architecture, planning and preservation. — 2nd ed.
     p. cm.
  Includes bibliographical references and index.
  ISBN 978-0-470-40464-5 (cloth :alk. paper)
 1. Architecture, Domestic—United States--Designs and plans. 2. Architecture—United States—
History—21st century—Designs and plans. 3. Housing—United States—Designs and plans. I. Kliment,
Stephen A. II. Chandler, Robert (Robert C.), 1954- III. Goody, Clancy & Associates, Inc., Architects.
 NA7208.2.B85 2010
 728.0973--dc22
                                            2009031415
Printed in the United States of America
10 9 8 7 6 5 4 3 2 1

CONTENTS

DEDICATION

to Joan Goody (1935-2009)

Joan Goody was our mentor, our partner, and our friend. Someone who loved the act of design, Joan encouraged a generation of architects to understand their civic responsibility for respecting the past while celebrating the present. Drawing on deeply rooted convictions and fundamental confidence in them, she inspired her partners to pursue our own convictions. In the toughest of times, she offered warmth and honest advice. When the Boston Society of Architects honored her for a lifetime of achievement, people from many walks of life and from cities across America came forward to thank Joan for endowing Boston, and her beloved profession of architecture, with a greater sense of humanism and civility.

PREFACE

Wiley's Building Type Basics series, conceived more than a decade ago by the late
Stephen A. Kliment, FAIA, series founder and editor who had served as editor in
chief of *Architectural Record* magazine from 1990 to 1996, includes one book on each
of the major building types that architects design.

Early in the development of the series, Kliment called upon expert architects, to
each author a volume based on the typology that they had built a career or firm upon.

Whom is this series intended for, and what purpose will it serve in your practice?
Building Type Basics books are written primarily for architects—from recent
graduates working on their first project in a building type, to experienced architects
who want the latest information on a building type they already know, to seasoned
associates and principals looking to add a new building type to their firm's portfolio.
Beyond architects, the series is useful to developers, builders, clients, urban planners
urban designers, and related professional consultants working with a given building
type. As Kliment had written in the preface to the first editions of the Building Type
Basics series: "As architectural practice becomes more generalized and firms pursue
and accept commissions for a widening range of building types, the books in this
series will comprise a convenient, hands-on resource providing basic information on
the initial design phases of a project and answers to the questions design professionals
routinely encounter in those crucial early phases."

Each volume of the Building Type Basics series covers what architects need to
know about the unique features of a given typology—from site selection and site
planning issues related to landscape and parking to predesign programming, project
delivery processes, building codes and accessibility, engineering systems, lighting and
acoustics, wayfinding, costs, feasibility, financing, and more. The latest editions in this
series, including this volume, offer information about sustainable design solutions, the
contemporary design trends related to that building type, as well as the most current
updates in both information technology and building technology that impact a
building type.

Case studies of the best contemporary projects of a given building type help to
illustrate the concepts presented in each book. Selected projects are geographically
diverse across North America and vary in scale so that one can glean lessons from a
given case study that can be applied to the architect's or designer's own work, whether
a small-scale project in a remote setting in a southern climate or a large-scale building
in a dense, urban setting in a harsh northern climate or somewhere in-between. That

is, wherever your project is located and whatever its scale, the case studies in this book offer valuable lessons.

Richly illustrated with diagrams, drawings, and photographs, the Building Type Basics series—through both visual information and narrative—will serve as both a guide and reference with its presentation of relevant concepts, design principles, and techniques to guide your projects.

John E. Czarnecki, Assoc. AIA
Senior Editor, Architecture and Design
John Wiley & Sons

ACKNOWLEDGMENTS

The authors wish to thank the people who helped this book come into being.

At Goody Clancy and Associates, Jennifer Gaugler carried on the work begun in the first edition by Jean Lawrence, helping to write new material and select new case studies and illustrations. Her research and her judgment were invaluable. Steve Wolf has refined many of the diagrams used to explain key concepts and enhanced many of the chapter and case study illustrations. Others at the firm contributed photographs and their expertise in specific areas.

Finally, thank you to the planners, architects, engineers, developers, government employees, construction workers, and community groups who contributed to the outstanding housing developments shown in this book. The hard work and skills of thousands of participants have moved the field of housing forward and helped create communities that are good places to live.

CHAPTER 1

INTRODUCTION

This book addresses the most typical living arrangements in the United States and many other industrialized countries, from the freestanding house to the high-rise apartment building. The authors are architects and planners who have designed and planned a variety of residential communities. They will explain what they believe makes "a good place to live" and how this has been accomplished with different housing types in settings ranging from rural to urban.

THE CONCEPT OF COMMUNITY

The focus of the book is not unique, single-family, custom-designed houses but, rather, groups of associated dwellings that form successful communities and serve as useful models for planners, architects, and developers working on larger projects. We are concerned with the individual dwelling—its functionality, buildability, and appearance—

Successful communities come in all forms and settings: a tree-lined neighborhood in Abacoa, Florida (right); a pedestrian-friendly street in the townhouse community of Hearthstone Mews in Alexandria, Virginia (bottom left); and a view from the river of Battery Park City in New York City (bottom right). Abacoa designed by DiVosta Homes; photo by Goody Clancy. Hearthstone Mews by Torti Gallas and Partners, CHK; photo by Richard Robinson. Battery Park City, photo by Philip Dyer.

▲ *Street-level commercial space at the base of mixed office and residential mid-rise housing at The Heritage, Boston, enlivens the neighborhood and serves building residents. The Architects' Collaborative. Photo by Goody Clancy.*

design a community in the smallest as well as the largest project.

Communities differ widely depending on their traditions, location (whether urban or rural), and demographics (e.g., individuals or families). We believe that density (the number of households accommodated per acre) is a key to the character of a community. This book, therefore, is organized by housing types from least to most dense, from the single-family house to the high-rise building (Chapters 3 through 6). Our experience shows that a mixture of housing (and thus family household) types makes for a more lively community in most cases, and therefore this book emphasizes mixed-use and mixed-type communities. *Mixed use* refers to the proximity of residential development to schools, shops, workplaces, and cultural sites, a pattern often found in traditional small towns and cities. What constitutes mixed use can range from shops at street level in a large apartment building to the introduction of residential buildings into a shopping and commercial development to new town development with these activities located close to one another.

Mixed-type housing refers to developments that include a range of dwelling unit types that appeal to different kinds of occupants, such as studio apartments, flats, and detached homes. Many communities are both mixed-use and mixed-type.

and the way these dwellings when aggregated create whole streets, neighborhoods, and communities. We believe that balancing private and public space creates a good place to live. A large, luxurious house in a hostile environment can become a fortress and a prison for its occupants, just as the most beautiful public amenities cannot compensate for inadequate shelter. Chapter 2, "Housing and Community," discusses the elements that make a successful residential community.

The type and quantity of shared amenities planned for a residential community depend on the number of residents who share (and can therefore support) them. These amenities might include recreation and play areas, as well as libraries, schools, and shops. Someone building fewer than 50 new homes (whether freestanding or in an apartment building) will not be able to provide as many communal facilities as the developer of 500 or more units. But there are ways to

SPECIALIZED HOUSING TYPES

This book does not cover housing types developed specifically for the elderly (retirement or assisted living) or the young (student housing). Both of these segments of the population, however, can make vital contributions to the life of any community and should be considered in mixed-type and mixed-use developments. Elderly people and students tend to be out on the street at times when the working population is not (midday and evenings, respectively) and both enliven and benefit from downtown locations that may appeal less to families with children.

Starting with the example of the Savannah College of Art and Design, which moved into a series of renovated historic buildings in downtown Savannah, Georgia, in 1979, colleges and cities have come to see the reuse of older buildings (department stores for classrooms, outmoded office spaces for dormitories) as opportunities to repopulate deserted downtowns. Similarly, unused, older downtown hotels and neighborhood elementary schools are often converted successfully into senior housing, providing places where downsizing elderly households can stay within their old neighborhoods and live close to public transportation.

Housing specifically designed for elderly and student populations is covered in other Wiley Building Type Basics volumes: *Building Type Basics for College and University Facilities* by David J. Neuman and *Building*

▲ *Community plaza at Mizner Park, Boca Raton, Florida. A new community hub can be created by adding housing and other uses to a failed shopping mall. Photo courtesy of Cooper Carry, Inc.*

◀ *The new town of Celebration, Florida, has a successful mixed-use town center. Cooper Robertson & Partners and Robert A. M. Stern Architects, master architects. Photo by Victor F. Ortale.*

▶ *The 1957 Monsanto House of the Future incorporated new materials and construction techniques in a prototype for mass-produced housing. Photo courtesy of Goody Clancy.*

Type Basics for Senior Living by Bradford Perkins (both published by John Wiley and Sons, New York, 2003). This book discusses the adaptive reuse of older structures for housing more generally (see Chapter 7, "Adaptive Reuse").

DIRECTIONS IN HOUSING CONSTRUCTION

While writing about the best housing practices of today, we also want to look to the future. What new ideas are on the horizon? Our firm, Goody Clancy, was established in 1955 to build a House of the Future for Disneyland in Anaheim, California; it was ultimately visited by over seven million people. Based on building materials research by the late Marvin Goody and others at the

Massachusetts Institute of Technology (under sponsorship of the Monsanto Corporation), the project explored the uses of plastic in housing. The dramatic forms of that housing took advantage of the particular qualities of plastic. It was one of a number of attempts by Goody Clancy and others to develop dwellings that could be prefabricated in factories and erected quickly and in large quantities under many different site conditions.

However, prefabrication (whether plastic, concrete, steel, or other materials) requires a large market within an economical shipping distance of the factory, something that is difficult to provide unless by a government client (as in the former Soviet Union). In the United States, prefabrication of flat

◀ At Kronsberg, a sustainable, mixed-use community in Hanover, Germany, storm water is collected in ponds. In the background, a residential building has movable sunscreens to control heat gain. Willen Associates Architekten. Photo by Karl Johaentges.

components (building walls, trusses, etc.) that can be shipped easily has traditionally been more successful than prefabrication of whole units. Manufactured homes, also known as mobile homes or trailers, have, however, become a staple of low-cost American housing. Mobile homes are built to separate codes and valued as personal property. Another type of prefabricated housing, modular housing, has seen significant market growth in the last decade. Modular homes are built in factories to the same codes as site-built housing, and they are often indistinguishable from site-built homes once completed. They consist of one or more modules narrow enough to travel along a highway and that can be expanded or combined on the site.

The exploration of new materials and methods of construction has continued since the mid-1950s with only modest changes in building methods and greater progress in new materials and the prefabrication of building components. Much of the current interest in new building materials has focused on those that are most sustainable—for example, recycled denim that can be used as insulation or compressed earth that can form a load-bearing wall. The Massachusetts Institute of Technology (MIT) is exploring ideas for new digital and building technologies that make domestic life easier (enabling people to keep house, shop, and manage resources, often from remote locations) and that help conserve energy through better controlling and monitoring methods. Their goal is to create responsive environments through sensing and communication media, ultimately making smart houses for everyone and in particular allowing the frail elderly to live more independently.

Conventional means and methods of building housing are still the most common and vary with the type (low-rise vs. high-rise) and with local conditions. Structural, mechanical, and other building systems share similarities across different housing types. We discuss these in Chapter 8, "Building Systems," noting specific variations for the different housing types.

Sustainable design in housing, as in all architecture, extends beyond simple energy conservation to a concern for all resources. It can be addressed in a variety of ways that include building near transit to reduce automobile dependence (as at Prairie Crossing, Grayslake, Illinois, a case study in Chapter 3); reuse of existing structures (renovation and adaptive reuse); use of recycled materials; and conservation of land and water.

We highlight these features where they appear in the projects selected as case studies.

FINANCING HOUSING

A house is the most expensive item that most people will ever own, typically absorbing one-third to one-half of household income when mortgage and other payments are counted. This heavy financial investment may be one reason that most buyers in this country choose a more traditional or historicist style over a contemporary one. Traditional designs are assumed to have a better resale value, and most developers are reluc-

tant to build for the estimated 5–10 percent of the house-buying public who prefer a contemporary modern style.

Financing plays a critical role in determining what is built and how it is constructed. The government subsidizes housing construction in numerous ways: tax deductions for mortgage payments (to encourage home ownership), tax credits for the reuse of historic structures (to encourage preservation), and direct subsidies to produce low-income housing for those who might otherwise be unable to afford to rent or buy a home. In Chapter 9, "Financing and Feasibility Issues," we address some of the typical means of financing housing—whether subsidized, market-rate, or luxury—and discuss the process of moving from design ideas to completed projects.

This book broadly covers many types and combinations of housing. Case studies of successful communities, drawn mostly from around the United States, illustrate key points about each housing type. The case studies do not represent a comprehensive survey; instead, they provide a small sampling of valuable examples. The bibliography will guide those who choose to explore any aspect of community housing and development more deeply. As we know, the study of housing is a lifetime project.

CHAPTER 2

HOUSING AND COMMUNITY

More than just the location of one's house, a true community provides opportunities for gathering, meeting, and making contact with neighbors at many levels—from over-the-fence pleasantries to group action for local improvements. Through its design, a community can foster an identification with the neighborhood and enrich the lives of its residents. Images of desirable places to live rarely show an isolated subdivision with thousands of identical houses lined up along unpopulated, anonymous streets. More likely we will see a neighborhood with a variety of houses (and often housing types), small squares or parks, and perhaps a Main Street with shops—things that strike a chord within many as the essence of community.

In this chapter we offer an overview of the tradition of community, note ways in which these traditions are changing, and suggest some core principles for designing and developing housing today.

BACKGROUND

People have made their homes in groups since the earliest times—for protection from hostile outsiders, for economic reasons (markets and the exchange of services), and for social reasons (conversation at the communal well or local pub). Groups of people living close together also make for more effective government—whether that government consists of a ruler who wants to keep an eye on the people or the citizens of a democracy meeting to agree on policies and actions.

By the mid-twentieth century, with the widespread ownership of automobiles in the United States allowing greater dispersion of housing, the focus of planning shifted from shared public

▼ A traditional American community in Vermont shows houses lining the main street. Photo by Joseph Sohm; © Joseph Sohm, Visions of America/CORBIS.

areas to extensive development of private realms. This private realm came to consist of the individual house and yard with, at most, semiprivate, shared swimming pools and play spaces but no relation to public parks, schools, shops, or public transit. These new communities not only celebrated the rise of the automobile but made it essential to daily life.

Late-twentieth- and early twenty-first-century advances in electronic communication have provided many more options for where and how we choose to live: we can telecommute to work and keep in touch via e-mail and social networking sites like Facebook. Internet retailers deliver goods almost anywhere. But the cost of these advances, in many cases, is isolation from a physical community with face-to-face contact. Although some people choose to live apart from any community, most do not.

Many housing communities built during the late twentieth century (and still being built) were intended for a relatively homogeneous population—all retirees, all families, or all people of a certain income level, for example. Sometimes these communities have walls and a guarded gate; sometimes they are just a group of homes with an internal street system that connects to the street system around them at a single point. Whether gated or not and whether in rural or urban settings, these communities respond to a desire to create an oasis in what is perceived as a hostile environment. They are designed to stand apart from their surroundings.

PRECEDENTS FOR CURRENT COMMUNITY DESIGN

Conscious efforts to make housing developments enhance the richness and variety in their community often follow the patterns of European villages and of North America's earliest cities, which produced eighteenth-century neighborhoods such as Boston's Beacon Hill and the planned blocks and squares of Savannah, Georgia. They also draw on mid-nineteenth-century efforts to plan complete new communities with their own parks, neighborhood commercial centers, and strong identities, such as garden suburbs like Lake Forest and Riverside, which grew out of the extension of rail service from Chicago.

Renewed interest in more traditional forms of community, organized around a strong public realm that deemphasized the automobile, began with proposals in the 1960s. One of the earliest developments was the Rouse Company's first neighborhood in Reston, Virginia, outside of Washington, D.C., which centered on a pedestrian-oriented neighborhood. Goody Clancy & Associates' 1978 design for renovating New England's largest distressed public housing project into a traditional mixed-income neighborhood (Columbia Point to Harbor Point) is another early example of such a designed community and was an inspiration for the Federal HOPE VI program, which provided over $6 billion for new housing nationwide in the 1990s and 2000s.

The New Urbanist movement, led by Andrés Duany and Elizabeth Plater-Zyberk, captured the imaginations of many, with projects like Seaside, Florida, developed by Robert Davis in the early 1980s. This project consciously evoked traditional community design principles and sparked interest among developers (and eventually elected officials) in creating new communities with a mix of uses and housing types. These communities share several characteristics: com-

pact town or neighborhood commercial centers with houses and other buildings facing the streets to promote walkability; a distinctive character established by design of the public realm (the squares and parks); availability of on-street parallel parking; and a connection to surrounding places via streets, views, and public transit.

At the same time, developments like Goody Clancy's mixed-income Tent City in Boston provided models for redevelopment in historic and traditional urban neighborhoods by demonstrating an alternative to much of the multifamily housing produced during the earlier period of urban renewal, which had ignored traditional neighborhood design qualities. Tent City places new row houses next to historic row houses, but another portion of the development rises to 14 stories along a busy commercial street, thus providing a mix of housing types while tying them to the surrounding urban fabric (see the case study in this chapter, p. 26).

Seeking to reverse regional growth away from sprawl and back toward the city core, planning during the 1990s and early 2000s in Portland, Oregon, and Seattle, Washington, introduced higher-density mixed-use neighborhoods, including loft apartments,

that have become models for redevelopment in many older urban and suburban neighborhood centers.

These higher-density neighborhoods depend on public transit, but automobiles have not disappeared from them. The goal is often to "tame" the impacts of high traffic volumes with narrow streets and curbside parking and to hide automobiles, when not in use, in garages below grade or behind wrap-around occupied space. The Portner's Landing development in historic Alexandria, Virginia, conceals cars in mid-block garages to minimize their impact on a historic community. The Museum Residences in Denver, Colorado, pursues a similar strategy: there, new residences and ground-floor retail wrap around a parking garage.

Celebrating and Separating the Automobile

A very different strategy, popular in the mid-twentieth century, was to celebrate the automobile. The road is a symbol of independence in the United States, and the influence of the automobile made itself felt in much twentieth-century development. "Carchitecture"—buildings designed to accommodate automobiles—proliferated: from the

▲ *Before and after the transformation of a public housing project into a new mixed-income community (Harbor Point, Boston). A new street plan, centrally located public amenities, and a combination of new and renovated buildings helped turn this community around. Photos by Alex S. MacLean/Landslides.*

▶ Daniel Libeskind's Museum Residences in Denver, Colorado, wraps around two sides of a five-story garage and roof garden, providing dramatic apartments and high-style architecture. © Studio Daniel Libeskind.

drive-in movie and drive-through restaurant and bank to countless strip malls along major roads. The power of the automobile's influence can be seen in the garage-dominated facades of many suburban homes.

From the 1920s through the 1960s, one strategy for dealing with issues related to the automobile was to separate pedestrian and vehicular circulation. The developers of Radburn, New Jersey, envisioned a town for the automobile age. Established in 1929, it featured a pedestrian-path system separated from the street system and void of any intersections with streets at grade level. The orientation of homes to walking paths and parks produced a walkable neighborhood— almost half of neighborhood residents currently walk to buy groceries (compared to 8 percent for a nearby unplanned community), although as families acquired more than one vehicle, Radburn's streets and culs-de-

sac became congested. Similar efforts to separate cars and pedestrians in urban areas sometimes led to underpopulated and unsafe walkways where crimes tend to occur. This suggests that separating cars and pedestrians may work in an upscale suburban neighborhood but can be dangerous in an urban setting.

When designing parking, it is important to consider how far people are willing to walk from their cars. In the 1950s Victor Gruen devised an influential model that worked well for suburban malls, but not on a larger urban scale—even though it was frequently adopted by urban renewal plans of the 1960s and 1970s. Under this model, cars arriving from roads and freeways are parked in garages located around a central pedestrian core. Some characteristics of Gruen's prototype, however, survive in "lifestyle centers," smaller suburban malls designed to encourage foot traffic between stores and often incorporating office space and housing. Lifestyle centers and some urban mixed-use developments are designed so that residents and customers can park their cars when they reach the development and not need to use them again until they leave. Indeed, shopping malls with residences, like the Natick Collection outside of Boston and San José's Santana Row, could be considered the most automobile-oriented housing of today: they offer ample garage parking—so cars are not forced into a historic downtown area where they do not fit—and walkable (and weather-protected) retail and dining choices. Many traditional, retail-only malls are dying and being abandoned—providing opportunities for adaptive reuse and incentives to mix uses, including residential and office space, in redevelopment.

Current Trends in Community Design

Recent years have seen a return to creation of communities with a greater diversity of housing (and thus occupants), more varied uses (retail, offices, recreation), and stronger connections between new development and its surroundings. Many developers are creating such communities today. This book documents recent examples of planned community housing from every region in the country—and a few other countries—that realize the goals of diversity, mixed use, and community.

Since the late 1990s, the housing needs and aspirations of Americans have shifted more rapidly than at any point since the suburban boom that followed the end of World War II. Evolving demographics, changing personal ideals, and a new perception of what constitutes real estate value are working together to transform the United States' housing landscape. The U.S. has moved from a mass housing market to "a nation of niches" (a phrase popularized by the Urban Land Institute). In 2008 more than one-third of all housing was purchased by single people (roughly two-thirds of whom are women). This represented more than twice the market share of families with children, a homemaker, and a single working adult wage earner, a group that had dominated the market for decades. As recently as the 1970s more than three-quarters of households in the housing market included children. As that proportion shrinks to less than one-quarter, millions of people who once felt compelled to live in remote suburbs are turning to urban and older suburban neighborhoods. Much of the change in housing demand is driven by increasing numbers of 25- to 34-year-olds as they buy their first homes, and by empty nesters. Both groups will continue to grow for another 15 to 20 years.

The consensus of ideals that once focused Americans toward a single suburban American Dream has dissolved into a multitude of aspirations. For many, a shorter commute would be a primary factor in choosing their next house. In regions with mature transit systems, 10 to 20 percent of all housing demand is now focused toward neighborhoods within walking distance of transit, far outstripping existing supply in these neighborhoods.

Research suggests that neighborhoods that invite walking, primarily located in cities and older suburbs, are now considered healthier than suburban neighborhoods by larger numbers of home buyers. An increased sense of responsibility for the environmental impacts of personal choices about consumption is also changing attitudes toward housing. This sense of responsibility has translated into support for communities that require less driving as well as buildings that use fewer resources.

Creating Community in the Midst of Diversity

For more than 50 years, the United States built cities and suburbs for homogeneous groups who found community in the churches and schools that served their neighborhoods. Paradoxically, in the diverse neighborhoods of twenty-first-century America, the shared institutions that served homogeneous populations of one religion or cultural background no longer serve to create community. While still neighborhood icons, they represent only the body, not the soul, of community. A local library or park (particularly if it hosts events of interest to a cross section of the community) may become the new meeting place, or it may be a local store that neighbors frequent and where they can post notices.

To reintroduce a genuine sense of community requires that architects, developers, planners, urban designers, and others adopt new skills and perspectives. As existing neighborhoods, older suburbs, and cities are retrofitted and failed strip retail centers and other opportunity sites increasingly are transformed into entire new neighborhoods, these practitioners engage people in exploring concepts that were once considered unnecessary (a wide array of housing options), unmentionable (density), impractical (a lively public realm), infeasible (mixed-use development), or unbelievable (mixed-income living).

Parks will draw families with children together, but chance meetings along streets, in squares, or at a fitness center or coffee shop also provide important opportunities for people of different ages to get to know neighbors who are likely to lead very different lives.

PRINCIPLES FOR CREATING COMMUNITY

Basic Principles of Urban Design

In *Urban Design for an Urban Century* (2008), authors Lance J. Brown, David Dixon (a principal at Goody Clancy), and Oliver Gilham propose five principles that merit particular emphasis, given the forces shaping twenty-first-century development.

- *"Build community in the midst of diversity."* Their first principle notes that "an age of increasing diversity and economic fragmentation" requires the creation of places that not only draw people together but actively invite people of all backgrounds and that emphasize the public over the private realm.
- *"Promote sustainability at every level."* Rather than limiting sustainability features to higher-priced options, this principle emphasizes the need to plan and design housing that attracts people at all income levels to live in compact neighborhoods that support smart growth and make mass transit feasible.
- *"Expand individual choices."* This principle urges more diverse housing options, specifically restoration of options about where and how to live, in part by building at densities that support transit, recreation, and greater choice in housing types.
- *"Enhance personal health."* It is essential to create "communities that support walkability and reduce reliance on driving."
- *"Make places for people."* The final principle stresses the importance of planning and design that respond to human senses and create a genuine sense of identity by

paying visible respect to history and nature. At the same time, it recognizes the innovative spirit that reflects the values of each place and era.

Taken together, these principles suggest a series of priorities for planning and designing housing and neighborhoods that promote a genuine sense of community. To plan new development that enhances a sense of community requires an understanding of development economics, historic preservation, the prerequisites for successful neighborhood retail—and sensitivity to a new development's future residents.

Strategies for Creating Community through Urban Design

Promote mixed use
Mixing places where people live, shop, work, and play fosters the kinds of informal interactions that promote a sense of community in diverse neighborhoods where traditional meeting places have disappeared. Attracting enough customers to support new or revived shops and services, however, requires either sufficient population density within a 10- to 15-minute walk, or an attraction that can draw visitors from outside the community. Given increasingly fragmented buying habits, few neighborhoods can fully support a Main Street on their own, so commercial activity must be visible to and accessible by a larger community (and, if not near transit, supported by adequate and well-designed parking).

Involving a skilled retail consultant can help ensure that a Main Street will be commercially viable and include places where people can congregate outside home or the

workplace (for example, coffee houses, restaurants, or pubs). Such "third places" (neither home nor workplace) are vital building blocks for community. Planned events and activities (such as street fairs and farmers' markets) can also help jump-start a new community. A mix of other uses can increase the value of housing and promote a sense of vitality (and personal safety) by ensuring that people are around for much of the day and evening and throughout the week. More efficient use of land and facilities (such as parking, which can be used by office workers by day and residents at night) allows a developer to locate shops, cinema entrances, and other uses at street level, which benefits them, while placing housing above the street, which improves residents' security and gives them access to available views.

Design livable densities
Creating neighborhoods that offer residents the opportunity to walk to stores and parks, to use transit instead of an automobile, and

▲ High-traffic street scene. Density plus shops, schools, houses of worship, and workplaces contribute to daytime street activity. Photo by Goody Clancy.

to choose from a variety of housing options requires planning new neighborhoods—or retrofitting existing ones—at densities that support these and similar enhancements of quality of life. One block of new Main Street retail (30,000–50,000 sq ft) requires 1,000 to 2,000 units of housing within a 10- to 15-minute walk. Providing this much housing involves reintroducing densities historically found in urban neighborhoods (40 to 100 units or more per acre) and associated, for example, with a mix of small-lot single-family houses, row houses, two- to six-family houses, apartments, and lofts.

Provide diverse housing options

A variety of housing options is necessary to accommodate diverse households: single-family houses, row houses, lofts, and flats in the same neighborhood serves people of different ages and family structures, with and without children. It also enables residents to age in their neighborhoods—as they move from family houses to single-level apartments.

Make connections to surrounding neighborhoods

A development isolated from surrounding streets and amenities deprives its residents of natural connections to the larger neighborhood, city, and region. Forging connections with surrounding neighborhoods begins with a street network linked to adjacent streets and buildings that relate to the character, uses, and scale of the surrounding area. Ideally, there will also be a choice of modes of transportation. Attracting outsiders also helps to support a vibrant Main Street.

Design a compelling sense of place

America's memorable communities—particularly those that have survived periods of ur-

ban decline—often embody a unique sense of place. Well-known historic examples of such places include Boston's Commonwealth Avenue and Denver's LoDo District. New communities such as Celebration, Florida, and A New Neighborhood at Old Davidson, North Carolina, also utilize distinctive public spaces to create a strong, highly marketable character.

Provide a choice of modes of transportation

Nearby public transit—whether subway, train, bus, trolley, or boat—will serve those who choose not to or cannot drive (including children, the elderly, or the disabled). Adequate but inconspicuous parking should be provided for both cars and bicycles.

With convenient and varied transit options, residents of a broader range of ages will populate the streets through the day. Varied modes of public transit will also attract outsiders who will help support a vibrant Main Street.

Create a vibrant public realm

Alexander Garvin notes that "Flexible planning requires a public realm that forms the armature around which healthy communities grow" (Gause 2002, p. 29). In most cases, the single most important element of that armature is a system of streets and blocks connected to parks and squares that conveys a neighborhood scale and character in keeping with local patterns. Together these streets, parks, squares, and similar elements provide the settings for the kinds of human contact that impart a sense of community.

Strategies for Creating Community through Housing Design

Design buildings that promote a sense of community

Housing, along with other buildings and spaces, should orient to streets, parks, and squares to reinforce the liveliness and safety of the public realm. Nonresidential buildings should interact with the public realm: opening large storefront windows along Main Streets, avoiding blank walls and lifeless parking structures next to public sidewalks, and employing design features that engage pedestrians. Even mid- and high-rise housing can help build a sense of community. These housing types can have townhouse units at their base with multiple front doors that give public sidewalks a more human

scale (e.g., Boston's Tent City, discussed in the case study in this chapter).

Housing units, of every type, should have a street address and a semiprivate zone between street and front door

The relationship between house and street or sidewalk is far more comfortable and successful if there is a transition from fully public street to fully private interior—for example, with a stoop or garden, or perhaps

▲ Public spaces in successful communities project a compelling sense of place: A New Neighborhood in Old Davidson, North Carolina (above left); City Place, Florida (top right); Commonwealth Avenue, Boston (above right). Photos by Goody Clancy, Boone Communities, Goody Clancy, respectively.

a recessed patio with seating in front of multifamily entrances.

Provide curbside parking

Curbside parking is not only convenient but also contributes to a sense of shared ownership of the street and real security by populating the sidewalk with people coming and going from parked cars. The buffer between pedestrians and moving vehicles that curbside parking provides also serves to make pedestrians more comfortable and to calm traffic.

▲ *Ferry transportation can relieve highway congestion and provide a pleasant commute in some cities. Photo by Goody Clancy.*

▶ *A proposed mixed-use, mixed-income development, Parcel 24 combines high-rise, mid-rise, and townhouses along a neighborhood street in downtown Boston, revitalizing its edge with cafés, shops, green space, and multiple residential entries. Illustration by Goody Clancy.*

Design to encourage observation of street life

Communities with "eyes on the street," to borrow Jane Jacobs's phrase (1961), are perceived as safer. Front porches, stoops, or bay windows overlooking public spaces allow increased observation of street life—more "eyes on the street." (See tables on following pages for more on the contribution of the public realm to a sense of community.)

Provide street-level doorways

In addition to eyes, multiple doors on a street make the street feel more welcoming, secure, and—studies have shown—more inviting. Residents in Cambridge, Massachusetts, stopped objecting to multifamily buildings in their traditional neighborhood when these buildings were redesigned to incorporate row houses with individual doorways at the street level in place of a single entry for anonymous tenants entering and leaving a lobby. The local residents got to

◀ A grandmother on the front porch keeps an eye on a Brooklyn, New York, neighborhood in the 1940s. Photo by Joan Goody.

know their new street-level neighbors, and developers report that these units have been the first to sell.

Planning tools and basic decisions can help achieve these principles. The tables below (pages 18–20) summarize and quantify some of these planning guidelines.

◀ "Eyes on the street," small front yards, sidewalks, and cars all encourage activity along the street and make it safe. Harbor Point, Boston. Photo by Anton Grassl Photography; © http://www.esto.com.

Considerations for Building Community

THE HIERARCHY OF PUBLIC REALM SPACES		
Public Realm Element	**Planning Issues and Design Issues**	**Dimensional Issues**
Neighborhood parks	Located prominently within a 10- to 15-minute walk of every housing unit; programmed with uses that appeal to people of different ages, backgrounds, and incomes; provide quiet areas with seating.	Ranging from one-half to one acre in highly urban areas to several acres in areas dominated by single-family houses.
Children's playgrounds and small parks	Located within a 5- to 10- minute walk of every housing unit; highly visible; equipped with seating and play areas. Play fountains are particularly effective ways to attract a wide variety of children (and their parents) in diverse neighborhoods.	From as small as 1,000 sq ft in dense urban areas to a quarter-acre or more in single-family neighborhoods.
Streets and blocks	Connect to existing "grid." Reproduce scale of nearby blocks; avoid superblocks (more than 400–500 ft wide or 300 ft long). Smaller dimensions are preferable. A variety of streets and blocks can convey special character. Carefully chosen street trees, paving, and lighting convey desirability. Where possible, provide a minimum of 8 ft of sidewalk and planting strip to accommodate street trees.	Where possible, provide a minimum of 8 ft of sidewalk and planting strip to accommodate street trees.
Front yards and porches	Create a consistent pattern.	Minimum front-yard depth 8 ft.
Private yards	Where possible provide yards for households with children, although in urban areas access to a park or shared play area accessible without crossing major streets is also appropriate. Minimum yard depth 15–20 ft (depending on height of houses).	Minimum backyard depth 15–20 ft (depending on height of houses).

HOUSING TYPES AND DIFFERING ISSUES IN PROMOTING A SENSE OF COMMUNITY

Housing Type	Typical Gross-Density Range*	Planning and Design Issues**
Detached (generally 1- to 3-family and 1-3 stories)	4–10	Low densities do not support Main Streets, frequent parks, and other features that promote pedestrian-friendly environments. More effective if mixed with other housing types.
Single-family row houses (generally 2–4 stories)	8–30	The higher end of this range, can support Main Streets and parks that promote walkable environments. (Note: some developers achieve densities of 35 units per acre or higher.)
Three- to six-family houses (generally 3–4 stories)	8–40	Larger scale can reinforce important streets, and parks can mark community gateways.
Multifamily row houses (generally 3–4 stories)	25–50	Higher densities support Main Streets and parks that promote a walkable environment. Mix of housing types supports diversity.
Low-rise multifamily (generally 2–5 stories)***	20-75	Similar to multifamily row houses; townhouse configurations at street level promote a sense of connection to surrounding community. Higher-density communities can support structured parking, reducing areas required for parking lots.
Lofts	25–40	Similar to low-rise or mid-rise multifamily housing.
Mid-rise multifamily (generally 5–15 stories)	40–120	Townhouse configurations at street level (to promote a sense of connection) can play an important role in supporting Main Streets, parks, and a critical mass of people, promoting a walkable environment and community. Requires structured parking, which frees land for other uses. Higher densities often require more expensive below-grade parking.
High-rise multifamily (generally 15+ stories)	60–200+	Similar to mid-rise housing.

*Units per acre, including streets. Density in most kinds of building and zoning regulations is defined as a ratio of built area to site area. For example, a floor area ratio (FAR) of two allows a building to cover an area twice the size of the site. Such a building would be more than one story and might be accompanied by a height limit of, say, four stories. The same FAR of two could be fulfilled with a building that rises to the four-story height limit but covers only 50 percent of the site.

Density in housing is also often measured in terms of dwelling units per acre (DU/AC). For example, quarter-acre lots for single-family houses lead to a density of four units per acre. We employ this measurement—commonly used by planners to describe housing—in the charts that follow because it can quickly identify which types of housing a developer might want to consider for a given site. For example, if a one-acre site costs $300,000 and the planner is using as a rule of thumb $30,000 per unit in land costs, he or she will want to think about housing types that can generate at least 10 units per acre.

Whether parking is on the surface or in a structure influences the number of units possible per acre, particularly for multifamily low-, mid-, and high-rise housing.

**A note about parking: Parking requirements for residential development range from zero (in a city like New York) to anywhere from one-half to three spaces per dwelling unit. The requirements depend on such considerations as: the kind of development (single-family to high-rise); location (country, suburb, or city); targeted buyers (income, age, expectations); local codes; site size; and proximity to public transit. On-street parking is generally the least obtrusive and expensive, but it is not always allowed or feasible. There is no simple rule of thumb for the quantity of parking to be provided, but the number and kind of parking spaces is a major decision that affects the finances, marketability, and design of every project. Parking is discussed in Chapters 2–6 in relation to different housing types and also covered in the case studies.

***Height for low-rise residential construction is generally limited by local building codes for wood or steel frames as opposed to masonry construction. While many jurisdictions effectively limit this height to four floors, others permit four levels of wood-framed construction above a single level of masonry construction.

HOW MAIN STREETS FOSTER COMMUNITY CONTACT

Uses: more than retail	While retail is usually thought of as the core Main Street use, cafés and restaurants make up an increasingly important part of the mix. Because neighborhoods alone generally cannot support their own Main Streets, one or more regional destination uses (e.g., a large and very popular restaurant; an arts cinema; a unique bookstore) are needed to draw people from the larger region to support the Main Street. Housing on upper floors is appropriate for elderly and childless households.
Achieving the right mix and size	A market study is required to determine the mix of minimum (and maximum) sizes for a commercial district. A two-sided block of shops and restaurants might have 30,000–50,000 sq ft of commercial space at street level, supported by 1.5–3.5 parking spaces per 1,000 sq ft in urban and older suburban areas and up to 5 spaces per 1,000 sq ft in suburban settings. A traditional village or neighborhood center might include roughly 50,000–100,000 sq ft. Smaller retailers can require roughly 1,000 sq ft, while destination uses might occupy 10,000–30,000 sq ft or more. While supermarkets often require 60,000 sq ft or more, a new generation of urban food stores can adapt to less than 30,000 sq ft.
Planning and design issues: the value of street-level activity	It is usually very difficult to support retail or related uses on upper floors or in basements; these uses should be located at street level. Studies have shown that breaks of more than 50–100 ft between stores can discourage pedestrians from continuing along the street. Stores should line the street, with off-street parking behind them. Many very successful traditional Main Streets, like West Hartford, Connecticut, work this way. Pedestrian and vehicular connections to nearby residential blocks should be very convenient and well-lit to encourage evening use. Main Streets benefit greatly from public squares or other place markers that symbolize civic status and provide amenities and activities.

THE HIERARCHY OF STREETS AND PEDESTRIAN PATHS*

Street Type (from minor to major)	Number of Traffic Lanes	Street Width (FT)	Sidewalk Width (FT)**	Curbside Parking
Pedestrian paths***	0	8–16	None	None
Alleys	1–2	12–24	None	No
Neighborhood residential streets	2 lanes plus parking	38–42	5–8	For convenience; keep pedestrians on the street; to slow traffic
Neighborhood commercial streets	2 lanes plus parking	40–44	8–12	To support retail
Downtown streets	2–4 lanes plus parking	42–68	8–16+	To keep pedestrians on the street; to slow traffic

*Within any community the size of each street should be related to the activities surrounding it—from a residential street with single-family houses to a commercial street with through traffic.
**Does not include planting strips, often an additional 6–12 ft.
***Generally better accommodated as public sidewalks; may be desirable for important connections where streets are inappropriate.

CASE STUDIES

Harbor Steps
Seattle, Washington

The completion of Harbor Steps Apartments culminated a 25-year effort to develop a new urban neighborhood anchored by high-rise living units in downtown Seattle. When the development process began in 1975, this kind of community was uncommon in Seattle.

Centering the project are the Harbor Steps staircase and park, which connect the cty's waterfront and downtown. They enliven an eight-block-long corridor that had endured decades of decline. Mixed-use development—including high-end rental units, public recreational areas, museums, office and retail space—has also helped in the revitalization of the neighborhood.

Program
The vision for Harbor Steps Apartments was a high-density urban development, resembling a European neighborhood, with a mix of restaurants, shops, and residences. To provide enough population to support these uses (to create what planners call a "critical mass"), a large number of dwelling units was required. It took the developer 20 years of consolidating contiguous properties and swapping land with other downtown owners to assemble a site large enough for the dense mixed-use development. Construction on the four towers and staircase park was completed in three phases.

In addition to 734 residential units, the Harbor Steps program includes a small boutique hotel, 30,000 sq ft of offices, an independently managed conference center, a day care center, and athletic facilities such as a

basketball court and a climbing wall. Sixty thousand sq ft of retail space, restaurants, and parks also serve both residents of the development and other downtown populations.

Planning / site concepts / parking
The terraced park and staircase at Harbor Steps dramatize the downtown area's hilly

▲ Pedestrians congregate on the feature for which Harbor Steps, Seattle, Washington, is named, with Jonathan Borofsky's "Hammering Man" sculpture behind them. Hewitt Architects. Photo by Michael Shopenn.

▲ *Harbor Steps is a mixed-use residential development of high-rise towers and public courtyards in the heart of downtown Seattle. Photo by Dennis Baerwald.*

walking to and from downtown offices and the ferry terminal, a block away.

The staircase is an active, urban gathering place for residents, downtown workers, and tourists, and it provides a platform for spectacular views of Elliott Bay. The quieter areas of the park, with fountains and terraced seating, provide a refuge from the noise and traffic of downtown Seattle.

Beneath the development, an underground parking structure separates vehicular traffic from the all-pedestrian site. Vehicular entry and exit to the garage are limited to a single location, further reducing the impact of cars on the development.

The exterior space around the towers forms both public and semiprivate realms. The public realm includes an eclectic mix of retail uses along the street, at the base of the towers, with canopies that extend over the broad sidewalks. Contrasting with these public spaces are more private residential gardens—the project's "backyard." Visible from beyond but accessible only to residents, the gardens form courtyards between the buildings.

Building design

Although the four towers differ from one another in specific detail and vary in height from 16 to 25 stories, they express a unified architectural vocabulary. The living units include lofts and flats and range from 450 sq ft studios to large penthouses. All unit designs emphasize daylight, views, and open floor plans.

Two overhead walkways link the towers and tie into the downtown public circulation system, further encouraging connections to the surrounding neighborhoods.

topography and strengthen its connection to the harbor. Inspired by Rome's Spanish Steps, the staircase connects the busy Pike Place Market, Pioneer Square, and Post Alley districts with downtown offices, hotels, and cultural attractions. The pedestrian path through this new development has become the preferred route for island commuters

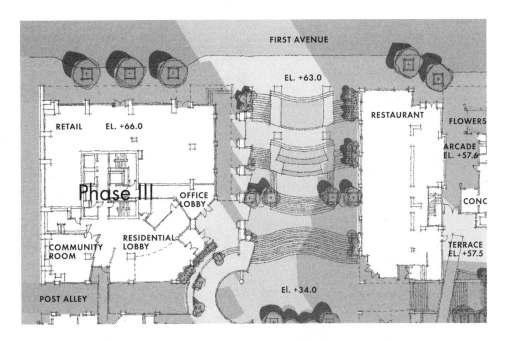

FIRST AVENUE

EL. +63.0

RESTAURANT

FLOWERS

RETAIL EL. +66.0

ARCADE
EL. +57.6

Phase III

OFFICE
LOBBY

CONC

RESIDENTIAL
LOBBY

COMMUNITY
ROOM

TERRACE
EL. +57.5

POST ALLEY

EL. +34.0

◀ This site plan, focusing on the landscape elements and building footprints for Harbor Steps, depicts the division of space among residential suites, public restaurants and meeting areas, and outdoor public space. Hewitt Architects.

◀ Aerial view of the towers at Harbor Steps and the city piers. Hewitt Architects. Photo by Michael Shoppen.

HOUSING AND COMMUNITY

▷ A view north through the Harbor Steps courtyard illustrates the project's synthesis of open space and high-rise towers. Hewitt Architects. Photo by Michael Shoppen.

▽ Post Alley, connected to Harbor Steps, is a pedestrian area defined by walkways and shops. Photo by Hewitt Architects.

◢ Sculptural elements and arbors punctuate and enclose courtyard areas at Harbor Steps. Hewitt Architects. Photo by Michael Shoppen.

HARBOR STEPS, Seattle, Washington

Owner / developer: Harbor Properties, Inc.

Architect:

Phase one: Hewitt Architects, Inc. (design architect); Callison Architecture, Inc. (architect of record)

Phases two and three: Hewitt Architects, Inc.

Landscape architecture, all phases: Hewitt Architects, Inc.

Contractor: McCarthy Building Corporation/SDL

Key consultants:

Landscape: Arthur Erikson

Structural: ABKJ

Mechanical / Electrical: 3DI

Civil: Magnusson Klemencic

Interiors: Marcia Johnson Interior Design; GGLO Interior Design

Project description: High-density, high-rise, mixed-use residential development in the central business district of downtown Seattle, Washington.

Completion date: 1997

Number of units / type / size:

734 apartments

31,000 sq ft of office space

25-room boutique hotel

51,600 sq ft of retail space

7,500 sq ft state-of-the-art conference center, restaurants, and specialty retail space

Site size: 2.26 acres (98,406 sq ft)

Density: 294 residential units per acre

Parking: 282,000 sq ft of subsurface parking for 640 cars

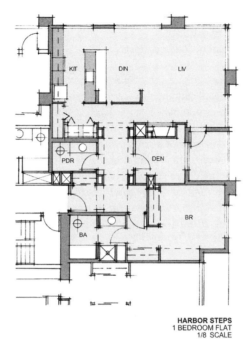

HARBOR STEPS
1 BEDROOM FLAT
1/8 SCALE

◀ *Floor plan for a small penthouse unit in Harbor Steps with a view oriented to the south and west. The entry procession was carefully composed to terminate each corridor with an "art wall." The final step of the route opens to an expansive view of Elliott Bay. Hewitt Architects.*

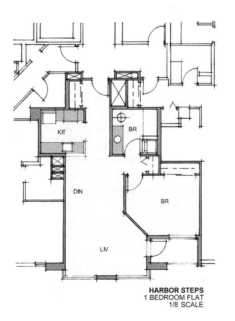

HARBOR STEPS
1 BEDROOM FLAT
1/8 SCALE

◀ *Floor plan for a one-bedroom flat at Harbor Steps. Few units in this downtown high-rise are typical. This one-bedroom has a view to the outside that expands dramatically at the transition from dining to living spaces. Hewitt Architects.*

Tent City
Boston, Massachusetts

Tent City is a mixed-use urban community. Its name commemorates a campaign of protests launched in the late 1960s by neighborhood activists, who camped on the site to prevent a large commercial development from replacing housing demolished during urban renewal. Twenty years of perseverance and active public participation resulted in the achievement of the activists' goal: affordable neighborhood housing on the site.

Program
Of Tent City's 269 living units, 75 percent are set aside for low- and moderate-income households and the other 25 percent are rented at market rates. The complex also incorporates 7,500 sq ft of commercial space, community meeting space, and day care fa-

cilities. Retail at the community's perimeter, including a neighborhood convenience store, serves both tenants of Tent City and the surrounding community; specialty stores face comparable retail establishments in the adjacent Copley Place development. The retail and housing both benefit from this mix: Tent City residents and the public support the retail, while the retail generates desirable activity around the housing.

The housing, shops, and interior landscaped courtyards are built on an underground garage with 698 bays, 569 of which serve the nearby retail and office development, Copley Place. The balance serves Tent City residents along with 17 on-street parking spaces. The proximity of public transit reduced the need for resident parking.

Planning and design concept
The overriding goals of both the planning and architecture of Tent City were to create a human-scaled urban living environment, to carefully meld new construction into an existing historic urban fabric, to achieve richness and variation within the constraints of severe budget limitations, and to demonstrate that outstanding residential quality and design need not be limited to high-end market housing.

In its materials and massing, Tent City makes a successful transition from Boston's historic Copley Square—with its large-scale churches, the Boston Public Library, and the more recent commercial complex of Copley Place—to the traditional Victorian townhouses of the historic South End neighborhood.

The twelve-story mid-rise building matches the height of Copley Place, then steps down gradually to four-story townhouses to meet its South End neighbors.

▼ Aerial photograph of Tent City (foreground) in Boston, showing how the buildings step down to make the transition from high-rise commercial development to the smaller townhouse scale of the South End. Goody Clancy. Photo by Steve Rosenthal; © Steve Rosenthal.

The curving northern face of the complex follows the path of adjacent underground rail tracks and a ground-level park built atop the trench through which the tracks run. Yarmouth Place, a new street within the site, was introduced to continue the adjacent street pattern and to reinforce the traditional street-building, wall-entry relationships, including on-street parking that augments the residential spaces in the garage. The site plan deploys buildings along the streets to create three sheltered interior courtyards with private patios and semipublic lawns, recalling the great Victorian squares found elsewhere in the South End.

The planning and architectural treatment attempt to reinterpret, not reproduce, features of the historic context in a contemporary vocabulary. These features include the residential scale and form, the entrance-to-street

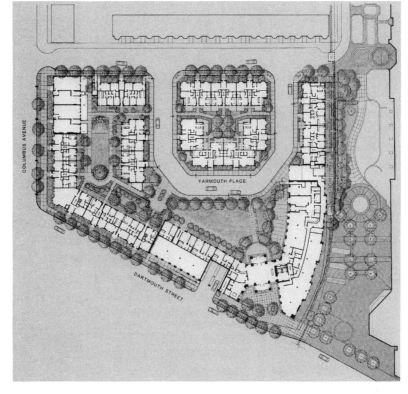

▼ Section through the townhouses and the parking garage under the housing and courtyards of Tent City. The stepped mid-rise building is in the background. Goody Clancy.

SITE SECTION

▲ Site plan of Tent City, Boston. The new mid-rise building with commercial space at its base adjoins the large-scale commercial area (right) and busy Dartmouth Street (bottom). Smaller-scale townhouses occupy parts of the site adjacent to surrounding townhouse neighborhoods (left and top)—note the large, semiprivate outdoor courtyards and the new loop street of Yarmouth Place. Goody Clancy.

▲ New townhouses against the backdrop of commercial buildings in Boston's Back Bay. Goody Clancy. Photo by Steve Rosenthal; © Steve Rosenthal.

◥ Courtyard with townhouse and mid-rise buildings. Photo by Steve Rosenthal; © Steve Rosenthal.

▶ The massing, forms, and scale of the low-rise section tie the development to its neighborhood context. Employing a contemporary vocabulary, they echo adjacent historic architecture without reproducing it. Goody Clancy. Photo by Steve Rosenthal; © Steve Rosenthal.

◀ An interior courtyard showing the private patios off the semiprivate seating space. Goody Clancy. Photo by Steve Rosenthal; © Steve Rosenthal.

▼ First- and second-floor plans of stacked duplexes in Tent City townhouses. Three- and four-bedroom units have kitchens and dining areas that open to private patios overlooking the shared courtyard. Goody Clancy.

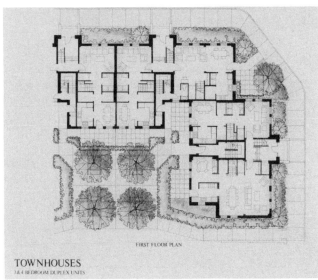

FIRST FLOOR PLAN

TOWNHOUSES
3 & 4 BEDROOM DUPLEX UNITS

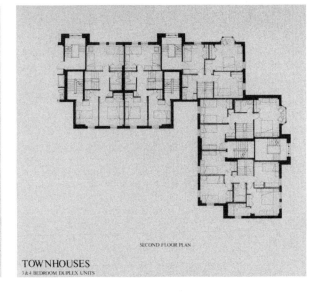

SECOND FLOOR PLAN

TOWNHOUSES
3 & 4 BEDROOM DUPLEX UNITS

▶ *Dining and living room of a townhouse unit at Tent City. The level change between living and dining areas creates a dramatic interior feature and conceals the basement parking level from view at street level. Goody Clancy. Photo by Steve Rosenthal; © Steve Rosenthal.*

relationship, the more private rear yards, the variety and richness of brick color and texture, the bay windows, and the entry design.

The buildings are clad in red and tan brick accented by colored glazed brick and precast concrete lintels. Changes in the brick color add interest and demarcate a distinct base, middle, and top to the buildings, as in traditional architecture.

Unit design

The all-rental dwelling units are accommodated in two building types: townhouse style, containing a combination of duplexes and flats, and the stepped mid-rise building, containing all flats (some of which open di-

rectly to the Yarmouth Place court). All large family units (three and four bedrooms) are duplexes in the townhouses, and they have private street entries and direct rear access to private exterior patios and the larger courtyards beyond.

Perimeter units take advantage of a grade change at the exterior edges of the underground garage to provide higher ceilings and step-down living rooms. One- and two-bedroom units in the mid-rise building have large bay windows with striking views of the city. True to the original intent, Tent City is integrated in all respects; there is no distinction in dwelling unit type, size, or location relative to income.

Financing and development

Tent City was developed by a community-based nonprofit corporation (for the housing and retail) in cooperation with a private developer (for the below-grade parking). Its innovative financial structure included 8 sources of seed money to finance initial development costs and 14 sources of permanent financing and rental assistance. The project is a testimonial to the determination of community activists to preserve economic and racial diversity in their neighborhood; to the cooperation among neighborhood groups, private developer, and city government; to the support of local and regional governments for affordable housing; and to the ability of nonprofit organizations to structure, design, finance, build, and manage high-quality real estate projects.

TENT CITY, Boston, Massachusetts

Owner / Developer:
>   Tent City Corporation (housing and retail)
>   JMB/Urban Development (underground parking)

Planner / Architect: Goody Clancy and Associates
Contractor: Turner Construction Company
Key consultants:
>   Development: The Community Builders
>   Structural: Zaldastani Associates
>   Mechanical: CA Crowley
>   Landscape: Halvorson/Moreice and Gary

Project description: Urban mixed-income community
Completion date: 1990
Number of units / type / size: 269 units
>   Studio: 1
>   One-bedroom: 93
>   Two-bedroom: 92
>   Three-bedroom: 66
>   Four-bedroom: 17

Site size: 140,180 sq ft
Density: 84 units per acre
Floor area ratio: 2.3
Parking: 698 spaces in below-grade structure, of which 129 are assigned to residents (in addition to 17 parking spaces on private Yarmouth Place). (Note: Proximity to rapid transit reduced the need for resident parking.)

Mizner Park
Boca Raton, Florida

Mizner Park is a new town center district in Boca Raton, Florida. The project sparked the wider revival of a fading downtown by replacing a failed regional shopping mall (dating from 1974) with a new mix of uses. Its planning concepts and architectural vocabulary draw on the Spanish colonial traditions of Florida.

In its rethinking of an ailing regional mall on a 28-acre site, Mizner Park provides a model for the redevelopment potential inherent in many U.S. retail centers that replaced town centers but have themselves fallen upon hard times.

Program
A monumental central outdoor space and new uses co-exist in this 24-hour new town center. Mixed-use buildings integrate office and retail space, apartments and townhouses, cinemas, restaurants, a museum, and a performance complex. On-street parking and adjacent structures accommodate parking for 2,500 cars.

Planning / site concepts
A key planning concept for Mizner Park was the organization of the community around a grand, formal public space, the Plaza Real.

Defined by four mixed-use buildings, the central space is lined with street-level arcades. With two-thirds of the site designated as public space and the site's ease of access by car or on foot, Mizner Park attracts the level of activity—the critical mass—needed for a major Main Street.

▶ Mizner Park, a cultural, civic, retail, and residential complex in Boca Raton, Florida, is laid out on a colorful carpet of paving stones that range from terra-cotta to charcoal gray. The fountain is one of several gathering places in the central village. Its decorative columns were cast from some of Addison Mizner's original molds. (Mizner, an architect, pioneered the Mediterannean revival style popular in South Florida and launched the development of Boca Raton in the 1920s.) Cooper Carry, Inc. Photo by Stephen Traves; © Stephen Traves Photography.

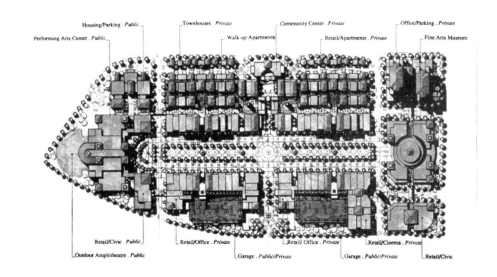

Housing/Parking . *Public*

Performing Arts Center . *Public*

Townhouses . *Private*

Walk-up Apartments

Community Center . *Private*

Retail/Apartments . *Private*

Office/Parking . *Private*

Fine Arts Museum

Retail/Civic . *Public*

Outdoor Amphitheatre . *Public*

Retail/Office . *Private*

Garage . *Public/Private*

Retail/ Office . *Private*

Garage . *Public/Private*

Retail/Cinema . *Private*

Retail/Civic

◀ *The master plan for this 28.7-acre center included four main mixed-use buildings situated around a village green. Mizner Park is anchored at each end by public uses—a museum and an amphitheater. Cooper Carry, Inc.*

◀ *A true mixed-use community, Mizner Park comprises residential apartments and condominiums that overlook street-level retail stores and entrances. Its ambiance represents a return to Main Street—a place where people can live, work, shop, and play. A broad village green runs through the middle of the development, providing a central place to gather and enjoy the company of others. Cooper Carry, Inc. Photo by Stephen Traves; © Stephen Traves Photography.*

▶ *Pedestrian and retail mall at Mizner Park. Careful attention to urban design issues and the intention of creating a sense of place make this project noteworthy. Its mix of uses and town center configuration (especially its restaurants and street-front retail, which borders a central public park) has stimulated vibrant, around-the-clock activity. Cooper Carry, Inc. Photo by Cooper Carry, Inc.*

First-floor retail and restaurants form connections between the public buildings that bookend the central space; the upper floors house rental apartments and office space.

Building design

The buildings are organized on 30-foot bays. Recessed and projecting balconies, cornices, and arcades further break down the scale of the buildings. These elements also help create a sense of place and unify the project, despite variations in building use and height. Terraced apartments create a variety of housing types and increase ocean views for east-facing units. Street-level gates and roof elements emphasize the entrances to courtyards and define the edges of the central public space.

▶ *Mizner Park streetscape with garden plazas and on-street parking. Designed as part of Boca Raton's unique town center district, these urban apartments play a critical role in creating a vibrant 24-hour location. Clustered around the grand outdoor Plaza Real, the apartments sit directly above street-level shops and restaurants, and the residential complex provides parking, concierge services, and a health club. Cooper Carry, Inc. Photo by Gabriel Benzur; © Gabriel Benzur Photography.*

◀ Mizner Park residential parking entrance. Each townhouse features a reserved and private single-car garage directly accessible from the rear of the dwelling unit. On-street parking is also available, strengthening Mizner Park's Main Street atmosphere, though most of the project's parking facilities are concealed in decks integrated into the retail and office buildings. Cooper Carry, Inc. Photo by Stephen Traves; © Stephen Traves Photography.

◀ The project includes five stories of residential space located above retail. No single-use, standalone buildings were planned, and all ground-floor space is occupied by stores or building entrances. The Mizner Park apartments comprise 248 one- to three-bedroom rental units. Cooper Carry, Inc.

Native plants, including palm trees and flowering vines, are layered over the Spanish-style architecture to create an integrated and distinctly Floridian character.

Development

The result of a major public and private effort, Mizner Park was completed in four phases over 13 years. Each phase incorporated the full range of mixed uses: retail space, restaurants, office space, entertainment, cultural centers, residential units, and parking.

- *Phase I:* 125,000 sq ft of retail and restaurant space, 90,000 sq ft of professional space, 136 apartments, parking structures, and an eight-screen cinema
- *Phase II:* A nine-story, 112-unit apartment tower, including a health club, rooftop pool, and parking, as well as 24 three-story townhouses fronting the street
- *Phase III:* A 40,000 sq ft international cartoon museum and an 80,000 sq ft department store
- *Phase IV:* A seven-story, 170,000 sq ft Class A office building, as well as the new Centre for the Arts at Mizner Park

MIZNER PARK, Boca Raton, Florida

Owner / Developer: Crocker & Company
Boca Raton Community Development Corporation
Teachers of New York

Architect / Master planner: Cooper Carry, Inc.
Contractor: Centex Rooney
Key consultants:
Landscape: Warren E. McCormick & Associates
Lighting: Jules Fisher & Paul Marantz
Graphics: Tracy Turner Design, Inc.
Fountain: The Fountain People, Inc.
Project description: Mixed use
Completion date:
Phase I: 1986–1989
Phase II: 1993–1995
Phase III: 1994–1997
Phase IV: 1997–1999
Number of units / types:
Phase I: 125,000 sq ft of retail and restaurant space; 90,000 sq ft of professional office space; 136 apartments, parking structures, and an eight-screen cinema
Phase II: a nine-story, 112-unit apartment tower—including a health club, rooftop pool, and parking—as well as 24-unit, three-story, streetlike townhouses
Phase III: 80,000 sq ft Jacobson department store and two-story expansion of structured parking
Phase IV: 170,000 sq ft seven-story corporate office tower with street retail and executive parking
Site size: 28.7 acres
Floor area ratio: 2.0
Parking: 250 street parking and 2,500 structured parking spaces with valet service

CHAPTER 3

THE DETACHED HOUSE

A single-family house separated from its neighbors by open space on all sides—front garden, side yards, and backyard—has long been the American dream.

Whether the fantasy is the family farmhouse (on vastly reduced acreage) or a mini-estate in the English style, the freestanding home with a picket fence has long been our ideal and accounted for 63 percent of total dwelling units in the United States in 2001 (U.S. Census Bureau, 2001). This chapter addresses planned communities with multiple single-, two-, or three-family homes, not one-of-a-kind custom-built houses.

Many neighborhoods of single-family homes are laid out, or platted, with standard-size lots along straight or curving streets. Each owner is free to build his or her own house to local zoning or subdivision design guidelines. These guidelines usually restrict height, dictate setbacks from the property lines, and recommend site coverage (i.e., floor area ratio, or FAR), as well as require a certain number of off-street parking spaces. Sometimes a subdivision will also restrict architectural style (for example, no flat roofs or all mission style), color, building materials, and more.

◀ *The ideal single-family American house. Photo by Goody Clancy.*

▲ *Aerial view of mass-produced, inexpensive housing. The development of Levittown, New York, was begun in 1947 to provide affordable suburban single-family homes. The first houses were built in the Cape Cod style on small lots and laid out along curving streets. Photo courtesy of the Levittown Public Library, Levittown History Collection.*

A typical single-family housing development also begins with subdivision of the site into lots that can accommodate houses that follow local zoning rules. But because a developer will have overall control and oversee design and construction of all the houses, there are opportunities for creativity in shaping lots and structures that can increase density and encourage or control variety to suit a particular image or market. As land values rise, housing developers have sought to reduce the size of the individual lot to increase the number of houses that can be built on a

given piece of land. The influence of a recent trend in planning called New Urbanism (the creation of walkable new communities similar to traditional neighborhoods) has also encouraged lots with narrow street frontage, houses with front porches, and sidewalks used to create lively streetscapes. These neighborhoods are fairly dense and usually contain communal open space.

As metropolitan areas grow, developments on the fringe are located farther from commercial and employment centers. Home buyers look for more services and activities integrated into their own communities. This has spurred a demand for mixed-use development, where offices, stores, restaurants, cultural attractions, and other services are incorporated into the neighborhood. In addition to amenities like bikeways and walkways, home buyers are looking for better access to public transportation.

BACKGROUND

Prior to World War II a typical single-family neighborhood had 50' × 100' (5,000 sq ft) lots with a single-car garage at the rear (reached by a driveway from the street). After World War II the typical suburban lot became wider to accommodate a two-car garage and larger overall (typically 10,000 sq ft or a quarter-acre)—although the pioneering Levittown (1947) development, on New York's Long Island, had 6,000 sq ft lots to keep costs down. House sizes grew steadily from a modest 1,100 sq ft, typical in the 1940s and 1950s, to 2,300 sq ft and more by the turn of the twentieth century. A recent trend toward smaller houses, to save both energy and cost, has led to *cottage* developments like Danielson Grove (see case study later in this chapter).

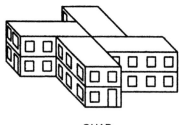

| SINGLE-FAMILY 1-3 STORIES | DUPLEX | SIDE BY SIDE | TRIPLEX 1 FLAT/FLOOR | QUAD FOUR TWO-STORY UNITS |

Levittown provided mass-produced, relatively inexpensive housing at a time of great need, but few would cite it for quality of site or architectural design. Earlier twentieth-century experiments in creating attractive housing developments in the new suburbs included Radburn, New Jersey (1929), and Chatham Village, Pennsylvania (1932–1936). These "ideal" suburbs reflected the influence of the Garden City movement, a European approach to planning that advocated self-sufficient satellite cities whose compact size would leave most surrounding land undeveloped. They represented an attempt to create whole new communities with shared open space and other amenities and with less emphasis on large, private lots.

These, and most other significant housing developments, have a mixture of housing types and sizes, and sometimes they aggregate several smaller units into what looks like one large house. This technique not only increases density and reduces price, but also creates houselike settings for smaller units and introduces smaller units into an area of larger houses at a compatible scale (see the case studies on La Brea Franklin Family Housing, p. 60, and Morgan Woods, p. 55).

THE BASIC BUILDING TYPE

The typical detached house has windows on all four sides, allowing a great variety of floor plans and windows in kitchens and bathrooms. Even when constituted as a duplex or fourplex, the detached house allows quite a few variations, since the exterior configuration is virtually unlimited.

Although less popular now, the two-family house (side by side or one above the other) has long been a staple of urban housing. Today the accessory apartment over the garage often serves the same purpose as the earlier two-family house—generation of rental income to make the house purchase affordable and to allow for future family growth. The traditional triple-decker (common in Boston and the older small cities of southern New England) has three levels of flats, each with its own front and rear porch.

Placement of the building on the lot is a key decision, frequently dictated by zoning setbacks. However, a fully designed project that reduces side lots but adds other amenities, for example, will sometimes qualify for zoning relief. The front-yard setback and character is often determined by local custom and culture. A well-maintained lawn has traditionally been the norm in suburbia,

▲ *Detached housing can be configured in many different ways.*

▶ In the new southwestern town of Civano, New Mexico, walls provide privacy for patios and reinforce the local vernacular architecture. Photo by Moule and Polyzoides; © Moule and Polyzoides, Architects and Urbanists.

but hedges and even walls at the lot line are acceptable in some communities. Concerns about water conservation and the large amount of water necessary to grow a lawn have led to more sustainable alternative planting schemes.

Many purchasers of detached houses expect a convenient indoor-outdoor connection to a ground-level yard or patio, although porches and decks are also desirable. Private outdoor space is typically in the rear, sometimes on the side, and less frequently in the front of the house. Occasionally, the design includes a fully or partially enclosed courtyard.

SITE DESIGN AND PARKING

A single-family housing development may be organized around straight streets or curving roads. When generated by hilly topography, curving roads make most sense, but they are sometimes used in an attempt to

achieve a rural flavor. The cul-de-sac road pattern maximizes privacy by discouraging through traffic, but this privacy generally comes at the cost of community.

Several questions must be addressed at the start of site design:

- *How does this development relate to its surroundings?* Should its streets align with surrounding streets? Should its houses face the public street, or should they be inward-oriented and disconnected from the outer community, as in a gated community?
- *How does each house within the development relate to the others?* Should the development afford maximum privacy and anonymity, or should it provide opportunities for contact with neighbors?
- *Will there be shared amenities: open space, natural features, or common facilities?* If so, should walking be encouraged to get

to them, by way of either sidewalks along the roads or a separate pedestrian path system?

Accommodating the automobile on a larger lot may be less of a challenge than getting two (or three) parking places on a 2,500 sq ft lot; but, in either case, making this accommodation well is critical to the appearance of a home.

Garages, porte cocheres, or even uncovered parking spaces may be accessed from the street or from a rear parking lane. Garage doors may face the street or be obscured; the garage itself may be set far back on the lot or closer to the street, attached to the house or not.

As noted, more activity on the street side, as neighbors come and go, yields greater contact and safety in the community. Even if the connection from garage to house is internal, vehicular access from the street instead of from an alley can contribute to activity on the street. On the other hand, garage doors that dominate the streetscape are not desirable. A good balance is achieved at Prairie Crossing (see case study, p. 48).

EXTERIOR DESIGN

The range of possible styles and materials is vast. Drawing on the local vernacular and common materials often makes good aesthetic as well as practical sense. Sloped roofs in wet climates and wide overhangs in sunny ones work with the weather, save energy, and look at home in their surroundings. In recent years, there has been an increase in the popularity of low-maintenance, durable exterior materials such as fiber cement and stone.

Given four exposed sides, orientation of large windows and outdoor spaces to the comfortable side (sunny in some locales, shady in others) and location of fewer openings in the direction of storms and wind are important. Views are also a factor, whether of fine scenery or away from a neighbor's property. When view and sun orientation conflict, the house is generally oriented for the view; creative design can lead to other ways of taking advantage of environmental factors.

Variety becomes more important as the size of a development increases. There may be variations from one subsection to another, as

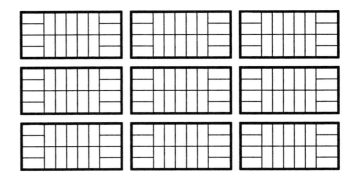

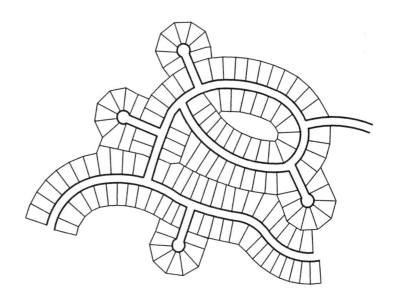

▲ Street-layout alternatives in single-family communities range from grid (above) to cul-de-sac (below) configurations.

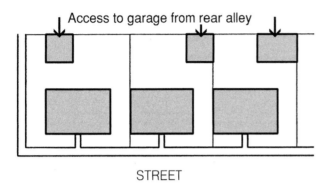

Access to garage from rear alley

STREET

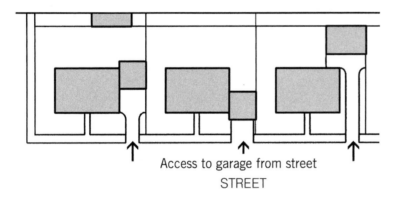

Access to garage from street
STREET

▲ *Garage-location variations for detached housing.*

large lot sizes (often required by local regulations), and in the Pacific region, because of a scarcity of buildable land. Foundations vary greatly by region: basements are found in more than three-quarters of new homes in the Northeast and Midwest, but the South and West have a higher percentage of slab-on-grade homes, and some homes have crawl spaces. Exterior materials also vary by region: vinyl is the primary cladding material in the Northeast and Midwest, but stucco is dominant in the West, and bricks are most common in the South. Decks are common in New England, whereas porches tend to be more common in the South and West (National Association of Home Builders, 2006).

RECENT TRENDS
Trends in single-family home development can be used to predict market demands in the near future.

The average number of square feet in a new home increased by about 50 percent from the early 1970s to 2006. However, as a result of rising energy costs, changes in lifestyle, a growing awareness of sustainability, and decreasing affordability relative to income, the trend has reversed. Since 2006, homes have been built with less square footage. This does not necessarily mean smaller rooms, but often means fewer of them. For example, a separate dining room is rarely used today and dining space can often be incorporated into the kitchen. Reducing a house's footprint can also mean using space more efficiently by using previously unprogrammed space (for example, putting cabinets under a staircase) or having furniture that can be tucked away when necessary.

More flexible floor plans and informal space are also in demand by home buyers. This in large part reflects changes in society;

well as within a single block. There is no reason why all roofs or all siding must be the same color in a development of 50 or 100 units, since no cost savings result from this practice. But subtle variations are often more harmonious than blatant contrasts in style or color. Distinguished older neighborhoods that have grown slowly over the years typically share a common palette of materials and colors but show engaging variations from one house to the next. Such an approach to the design of a new development can be enriching.

REGIONAL DIFFERENCES
The most expensive homes in the U.S. are typically found in the Northeast, because of

◀ At Prairie Crossing in Grayslake, Illinois, a garage is tucked behind the house, reducing its prominence while retaining convenience. Nagle Hartray + Associates. Photo by Nagle Hartray + Associates.

buyers feel less need for formal spaces like parlors and dining rooms. Home owners today often request home designs that incorporate multipurpose rooms and allow for future renovations (e.g., non-load-bearing interior walls accommodate easy alteration—or removal—of walls and changes in room layouts as the owners' needs change over time). They also request more storage—volume that used to go toward a cathedral ceiling may now be used as attic space. Another way to maximize living space is through the use of outdoor rooms and living spaces, such as decks, porches, and landscaped areas.

Increased accessibility is also a growing trend. As the baby boom population grows older and life expectancy increases, more home owners want a house designed for ease of entry, exit, and interior maneuvering. This includes providing an entry at grade level, making hallways and doorways wider, decreasing the number of level changes, and planning for future installation of grab bars.

Home owners also look for ecofriendly home designs. Two of the most commonly addressed issues are energy and indoor air quality. Popular strategies for improving energy efficiency include an increased focus on better insulation, such as adding extra insulation to the attic, and the use of more efficient heating methods such as geothermal heating and tankless hot water heaters. To ensure good indoor air quality, the use of "green" finishes—including paints and carpets that emit low or no volatile organic compounds—is preferred. Neighborhood guidelines (whether actual or implied) can make it difficult to incorporate some of the less common green strategies, like using bermed earth to insulate one or more sides of a house; however, it is possible to blend traditional-appearing street-facing facades with innovative environmental strategies.

CASE STUDIES

Danielson Grove
Kirkland, Washington

▼ *The 2.25-acre Danielson Grove site in Kirkland, Washington, was originally intended to have ten 3,000 sq ft houses, but instead it was developed with 16 cottages half that size, plus a common house and two courtyards. Garages and parking are clustered at one side so residents must walk through the community to reach their front doors. Ross Chapin Architects, www.rosschapin.com.*

Danielson Grove is a community of 16 single-family detached cottages with shared outdoor common space and a community center. The small cottages are intended for singles, empty nesters, and young households. Danielson Grove is at the forefront of a small-house movement that emerged in reaction to the McMansion trend of the 1990s and early 2000s.

Building design
The homes at Danielson Grove are designed to be compact yet feel spacious. A typical model covers 1,600 square feet, about half the size of most new homes constructed in the area. Even in such limited area, the typical house contains three bedrooms, three bathrooms, a living room, dining room, kitchen, laundry room, and sometimes even a study space. Innovations like a pull-down staircase for attic storage help to save space, while open floor plans, expansive windows, and built-in cabinetry give a sense of spaciousness. The homes were built to meet the 4-star rating of the Master Builders Association Built Green program, which includes measures such as increased insulation and weather sealing; energy-efficient appliances, heating, and lighting; and sustainable materials with low toxicity and high durability.

Site plan
In a small, tightly-knit development, it is important to consider both community and privacy. The houses at Danielson Grove are arranged to promote both. The site plan fosters community through the organization of houses, pathways, parking, and communal open space, while the individual house designs provide a necessary sense of privacy when needed. Large front porches encourage community interaction. Single-car garages are clustered along one edge of the property, so residents must walk through the development to get to their houses. Yards are small, but shared grassy courtyards and the community center building provide additional space for social functions. Living rooms and dining rooms face the courtyards, while private spaces are found toward the back of the house and on the second floor. Adjacent homes are arranged so that no window looks into a neighbor's bedroom.

Any rainwater that hits a roof is directed into a bioswale in each yard, and the overflow is channeled to a storm-water detention

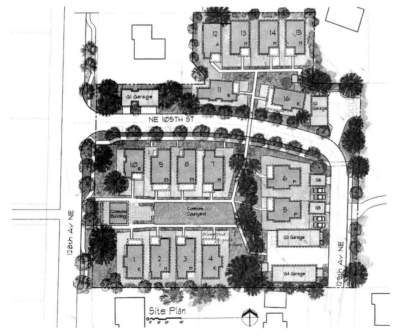

Site Plan

tank (which is important to protecting the water quality of the region's salmon streams). Existing coniferous trees were left in place during construction, providing shade and giving the development a feeling of maturity. Pervious concrete and gravel pathways allow rainwater to reach tree roots.

Development

Developers are responding to changes in the market; smaller homes can still be very marketable. This successful neighborhood resulted from the collaboration of state government, the city planning department, the developer, the architect, the banker, the builders, the land seller, and the home buyers. The architect and developer assisted the City of Kirkland in developing a new code that gave "density bonuses" if homes were

△ Cottages line the edge of a common courtyard, with the common house at the far end of the lawn. Photo by Ross Chapin Architects, www.rosschapin.com.

◄ Under the canopy of existing trees, walkways are made of pervious concrete or gravel to allow rainwater to reach the tree roots. Photo by Ross Chapin Architects, www.rosschapin.com.

First floor

Second floor

First Floor	
Living Room	12'-0" x 11'-6"
Kitchen	11'-6" x 11'-6"
Dining Room	11'-6" x 8'-6"
Bedroom 1	11'-6" x 10'-6"
Study*	7'-6" x 11'-0"
Bathroom 1	full
Bathroom 2	half
Covered Porch	11'-6" x 10'-6"
Second Floor> 5'	
Bedroom 2	14'-0" x 12'-6"
Bedroom 3	13'-0" x 11'-6"
Bathroom 3	three-quarter

Total Area "M" 1,552 sq ft
Total Area "M2" 1,456 sq ft*

* M2 plan does not include the study

▲ *There are six different floor plans in the Danielson Grove development. The typical square footage of a cottage is only 1,600 sq ft, but it includes three bedrooms, three bathrooms, a living room, dining room, and a front porch (e.g., this plan for a Madrona house). Ross Chapin Architects, www.rosschapin.com.*

limited in size, oriented around shared landscaped space, and had clustered parking. This new code allowed for the construction of an award-winning, highly in-demand, small-home community.

DANIELSON GROVE, Kirkland, Washington
Developer: The Cottage Company
Architect: Ross Chapin, AIA
Contractor: Jay Kracht, Construction Manager, The Cottage Company

Key consultants:
Structural engineers: Swenson Say Faget
Civil engineer: Triad Associates
Landscape: City Garden Services
Project description: Small-home community of detached cottages
Completion date: 2005
Number of units / type: 16 single-family cottages ranging from 700–1,500 sq ft
Site size: 2.25 acres
Density: 7.2 units per acre
Parking: 16 spaces clustered in garages on one side of the site

◄ *The Madrona is one of the six types of homes at Danielson Grove. A comfortable front porch allows residents to sit outside and interact with their neighbors. Photo by Ross Chapin Architects, www.rosschapin.com.*

▲ *View of the kitchen and dining room shows how open layouts and large windows allow small spaces to feel spacious. Fine detailing and quality materials also attract potential buyers. Photo by Ross Chapin Architects, www.rosschapin.com.*

▲ *Reading nook tucked into the landing of a staircase shows creative use of space. Photo by Ross Chapin Architects, www.rosschapin.com.*

▶ *Section through a typical Madrona house. Ross Chapin Architects, www.rosschapin.com.*

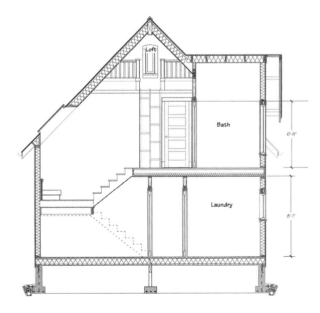

Prairie Crossing
Grayslake, Illinois

Prairie Crossing is a transit-oriented community located 40 miles north of Chicago. Designed in the 1990s, the project is firmly rooted in conservation principles. The development was initiated to provide an economic framework for protecting rolling farm fields and natural areas while also providing energy-efficient homes for the growing population on Chicago's metropolitan fringe. There are 360 single-family homes and 36 condominiums, as well as shops, restaurants, and a charter school, in the mixed-use development.

Among the goals that guided the development of Prairie Crossing are environmental protection and enhancement, a sense of place, convenient transportation, energy conservation, aesthetic design, and high-quality construction.

Site design
By clustering house sites along hedgerows, in small neighborhoods or villages, Prairie Crossing preserves as open land more than 60 percent of the 678-acre site. Each single-family house, while close to its neighbors, has views of open land, which ranges from small neighborhood greens to prairies, lakes, pastures, and farmland. Conservation easements legally protect the open space against future development, while a comprehensive land-use plan encourages development for sustainable and recreational uses. There are more than 10 miles of trails for hiking, biking, cross-country skiing, and horseback riding. In addition, 90 acres of the land are used for organic vegetable production and pastures.

▷ The houses at Prairie Crossing, outside Chicago, Illinois, were designed in traditional Midwestern styles and demonstrate the highest standards for energy efficiency of the U.S. Department of Energy's Building America program. Photo by Victoria Post Ranney.

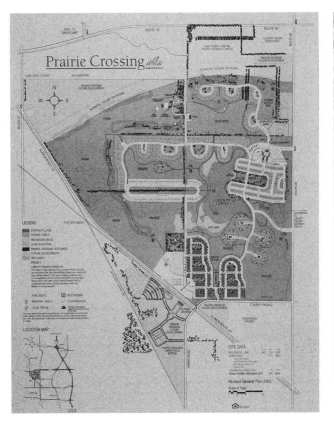

The site map shows the houses at Prairie Crossing clustered in two villages, in smaller neighborhoods, and along historic hedgerows, preserving over 60 percent of the site as farmland or natural areas. Shops and offices are planned near the crossing of two commuter rail lines.

Village Green homes at Prairie Crossing have rear garages with alley access. The Byron Colby Barn and the Prairie Crossing Charter School are in the background. Photo by Terry Evans.

Located next to the crossing of two commuter rail lines that connect Chicago and O'Hare International Airport, the Prairie Crossing site is designed to make walking and train travel practical alternatives to driving. Retail, office, and condominium development near the stations combines transit-oriented design with the conservation of open land.

Water management at Prairie Crossing takes advantage of the site's gently rolling hills, native plants, and natural water flow. Storm water flows off the roads and house lots into swales, then moves laterally through common areas planted with prairie and wetland vegetation. The long roots of the prairie plants (some as deep as 15 feet) hold soil in place and purify the water. Once purified, the water reaches a constructed lake that doubles as a swimming hole and a refuge for endangered fish.

Parking is accommodated in garages for detached homes. There is on-street parking in Station Village, and there are 78 spaces at the community center.

Building design

Eight architects have designed houses at Prairie Crossing in Midwestern vernacular styles, from farmhouses and foursquares to Craftsman-era cottages and Prairie School–inspired designs. The wide variety of

◀ Ten miles of trails wind through Prairie Crossing's open land, which is protected from development by conservation easements. All homes at Prairie Crossing offer views over some form of open land. Photo by Steven Arazmus.

▼ Lake Aldo Leopold was named after the Midwestern writer and educator who popularized the conservation movement in the mid-20th century. Its nesting island was engineered as an attractive habitat for fish, birds, and humans. A trail circles the lake and leads to a swimming beach. Photo by Victoria Post Ranney.

◄ At 1,478 sq ft, the Halsey model is one of the smallest houses at Prairie Crossing. It offers an efficient three-bedroom plan with pleasing proportions and clean lines. Tigerman McCurry Architects. Photo by Bruce Van Integer.

▼ Floor plans, first (left), and second (right) floors of the Halsey model, one of Prairie Crossing's smallest models. Tigerman McCurry Architects.

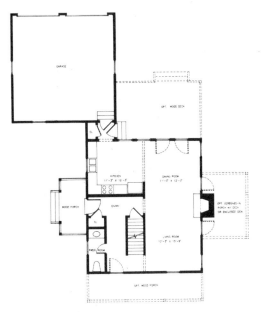

FIRST FLOOR PLAN
PLAN 1478

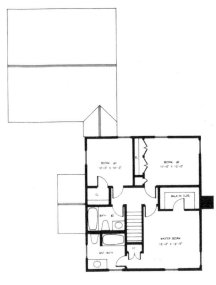

SECOND FLOOR PLAN
PLAN 1478

house sizes has attracted a mix of incomes to the community. Clapboards predominate as siding, and simplicity of line has been encouraged. Home buyers select the exterior color of their houses from a warm palette based on the prairie landscape.

The natural and human histories of the site are central to Prairie Crossing: much of its prairie land has been conserved for recreational use, and its buildings have been renovated as community space. An 1885 timber-frame dairy barn serves as a community center, and an old country schoolhouse has been renovated for the Prairie Crossing Charter School, a new public elementary school. The original farm buildings on the

▲ The Stevenson model, one of the largest houses at Prairie Crossing, is designed using a Midwest farmhouse vernacular. Nagle Hartray + Associates. Photo by Bruce Van Integer.

FIRST FLOOR

SECOND FLOOR

BASEMENT

▶ Plan of the Stevenson model at Prairie Crossing. Nagle Hartray + Associates.

◀ *The Byron Colby Barn, named for the local farmer who built it near Prairie Crossing in 1885. It now serves as the community center for Prairie Crossing. Slated for demolition in the 1990s, it was taken down timber by timber and reassembled on its present site, where it hosts community meetings, weddings, conferences, school events, and concerts. Photo by Hedrick Blessing.*

site now house a farmers' market, where residents and the public come to buy organic vegetables, eggs, honey, and flowers.

Building systems

Prairie Crossing was the first residential development in the country to adopt the systems approach and construction techniques of the U.S. Department of Energy's (US-DOE) Building America program for all of its homes. Efficient furnaces and windows are combined with a variety of building methods to increase energy efficiency. For example, 2 × 6 in. studs are spaced 24 in. apart (rather than the conventional 2 × 4 in. studs at 16 in. apart) to allow additional room for insulation in this extreme prairie climate. By USDOE postconstruction measurement, the Prairie Crossing houses are approximately 50 percent more energy-efficient than comparable construction in the region.

PRAIRIE CROSSING, Grayslake, Illinois

Owner / Developer: Prairie Holdings Corporation

Master planner: William Johnson, FASLA

Architects of single-family homes:
Margaret McCurry of Tigerman McCurry
James Nagle, Nagle Hartray + Associates, Ltd.
Frederick Phillips, Frederick Phillips & Associates
Betsy Pettit, Building Science Corporation
Howard Decker, The National Building Museum
Doug Farr, Farr & Associates
Mark and Linda Keane, Studio 1032

Architecture
Adam Shore, Professional Design & Associates, Inc.

Historic restoration architects:
Walker Johnson of Johnson Lasky
Gunny Harboe of McClier Corporation

Contractor:
Shaw Homes, 1992–97
Prairie Holdings Corporation, 1997–

Key consultants:
Applied Ecological Services
Calthorpe Associates
Arcadia Land Company
Peter Lindsay Schaudt Landscape Architecture, Inc.
The Schwebel Company

Project description: Mixed-use, transit-oriented conservation community of detached, single-family homes

Completion date: Single-family homes: 2005; commercial and condominiums: ongoing

Number of units / type / size:
360 single-family homes: 1,478–3,090 sq ft
36 condominiums: size to be determined
Retail, office, and commercial: to be determined

Site size: 678 acres

Density: Approximately three single-family houses per acre on the 135 acres reserved for houses. This clustering allows 470 acres of the site to be preserved as open land.

Parking: Overnight parking in driveways only for single-family homes, except in Station Village, where on-street parking is allowed. The community center offers 78 spaces.

Morgan Woods
Edgartown, Massachusetts

Like many seaside communities, Edgartown, on the island of Martha's Vineyard, has an economy that is driven by summer tourism. This creates a problem for a community when purchasing or renting a home becomes too expensive for local, year-round residents—who may be forced off-island in the summer due to high rental rates and limited affordable housing stock. Morgan Woods was developed through an initiative to create more workforce housing for island residents. The comprehensive permit was approved under the Massachusetts Comprehensive Permit Act, or Chapter 40B, a law that allows developers of affordable housing to circumvent certain municipal zoning restrictions and other requirements. Afford-

able housing is defined in Chapter 40B as a unit that could be purchased or rented by a household making up to 80 percent of the median income of the area. All of the units at Morgan Woods are rental units, and they are assigned by lottery to residents with a range of incomes.

Design
Morgan Woods comprises three clusters of buildings arrayed around a common open space. Each cluster reflects a traditional New England pattern of farmstead development, in which a barn and a farmhouse were built first, followed by additional buildings. Thus, each cluster has a red "barn" building that contains three two-story townhouses. Each also has a "farmhouse" with clapboard siding on the two-story portion. One-story "additions" on either side of the farmhouse are

▼ *Morgan Woods, Edgartown, Massachusetts, is designed to recall a traditional New England village that developed around a farmhouse and a barn, with additional buildings added over time. Photo by Bruce T. Martin; © www.brucetmartin.com.*

▲ The Morgan Woods development comprises 60 units within 21 buildings. The multifamily housing is designed to look like single-family homes. Photo by Bruce T. Martin; © www.brucetmartin.com.

◥Each unit has its own front porch and individual entry. Photo by Bruce T. Martin; © www.brucetmartin.com.

▶ Townhouses are located within a large red building that resembles a barn. Photo by Bruce T. Martin; © www.brucetmartin.com.

◀ *The first- and second-floor plans of a typical house show how three units are accommodated within one building. The Community Builders, Inc.*

PATIO

PATIO

PATIO

KITCHEN
(10x13)

KITCHEN
(10x13)

DEN
(12x13)

UP

UP

BATH

KITCHEN
(10x13)

DINING
(10x12)

BATH

LN

BATH

BEDROOM 1
(13x13)

BATH

PORCH

LIVING
(13x17)

BEDROOM 2
(11x13)

LIVING/DINING
(13x23)

LIVING/DINING
(13x25)

BEDROOM 3
(13x13)

PORCH

0   5'   10'   20'

PORCH

Typical 3BR Townhouse

Typical 2BR Townhouse

Typical 3BR Cottage

TYPICAL "MAIN HOUSE"

TYPICAL "MAIN HOUSE"

BEDROOM 3
(11x13)

BEDROOM 2
(13x13)

BEDROOM 1
(12x12)

DN

DN

BATH

BATH

LAUNDRY

BATH

BEDROOM 2
(10x13)

BEDROOM 1
(13x13)

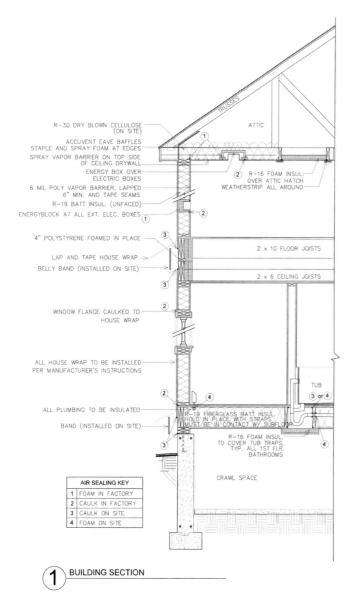

R-30 DRY BLOWN CELLULOSE
(ON SITE)
ACCUVENT EAVE BAFFLES
STAPLE AND SPRAY FOAM AT EDGES
SPRAY VAPOR BARRIER ON TOP SIDE
OF CEILING DRYWALL
ENERGY BOX OVER
ELECTRIC BOXES
6 MIL POLY VAPOR BARRIER, LAPPED
6" MIN. AND TAPE SEAMS
R-19 BATT INSUL. (UNFACED)
ENERGYBLOCK AT ALL EXT. ELEC. BOXES

4" POLYSTYRENE FOAMED IN PLACE

LAP AND TAPE HOUSE WRAP
BELLY BAND (INSTALLED ON SITE)

WINDOW FLANGE CAULKED TO
HOUSE WRAP

ALL HOUSE WRAP TO BE INSTALLED
PER MANUFACTURER'S INSTRUCTIONS

ALL PLUMBING TO BE INSULATED
BAND (INSTALLED ON SITE)

ATTIC

R-16 FOAM INSUL.
OVER ATTIC HATCH
WEATHERSTRIP ALL AROUND

2 × 10 FLOOR JOISTS

2 × 6 CEILING JOISTS

TUB

R-19 FIBERGLASS BATT INSUL.
HOLD IN PLACE WITH STRAPS
MUST BE IN CONTACT W/ SUBFLOOR
R-16 FOAM INSUL.
TO COVER TUB TRAPS,
TYP. ALL 1ST FLR.
BATHROOMS

CRAWL SPACE

AIR SEALING KEY	
1	FOAM IN FACTORY
2	CAULK IN FACTORY
3	CAULK ON SITE
4	FOAM ON SITE

(1) BUILDING SECTION

▲ The buildings have some structural characteristics that are unique to modular construction, such as floors of double thickness. The Community Builders, Inc.

clad in natural cedar shingles, as are the other buildings in the cluster. The buildings are designed to look like large single-family homes, but they all contain multiple units. Each unit has a front porch facing the common green. No two buildings in the development look exactly alike.

Construction
The cost of labor and of transporting materials to the island can increase construction expense by 25 percent. The architect decided to use modular construction to save time and money in the construction process. The homes were assembled in a factory and shipped on barges from the mainland to the Vineyard, as the island is known informally, where the modules were bolted together onsite. Because each module is a self-contained box, walls and floors are doubled in thickness—making the homes sturdy, quiet, and more energy-efficient but requiring more steel in the foundation, because loads are heavier. Construction of the entire Morgan Woods development was completed in 12 months.

Development
The Community Builders, Inc., developer of Morgan Woods, is a 501(c)(3) nonprofit affordable housing organization and the largest nonprofit urban housing developer in the United States. It funded the development through government subsidies, low-income housing tax credit equity, and private mortgages, and it holds a 99-year lease on the property from the town at the rate of $1 per year. Community Builders worked closely with the Edgartown Board of Selectmen, the town's affordable housing committee, the regional housing authority, local businesses, and many full-time residents to influence

zoning and assemble the permits necessary for this project. The town paid for the costs of connecting streets to the site and installing town water mains and wastewater connections.

MORGAN WOODS, Edgartown, Massachusetts
Developer: The Community Builders, Inc.
Architect: Winslow Architects, Inc.
Contractor: Williams Building Company
Manufacturer: Keiser Industries
Landscape: Horiuchi Solien
Project description: Modular development of multifamily detached homes
Completion date: 2007
Number of units / type: 21 buildings providing 60 units of one to three bedrooms
Site size: 12 acres
Density: 5 units per acre
Parking: 2.5 spaces per unit

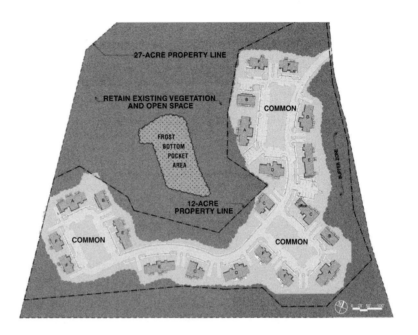

▲ Three clusters of housing units are arranged around landscaped common areas to promote a sense of small neighborhoods within the development. The Community Builders, Inc.

La Brea Franklin Family Housing
Los Angeles, California

Located at the base of the Hollywood Hills in Los Angeles, La Brea Franklin Family Housing consists of about 180 residents in 40 dwelling units. The units are grouped in 10 discrete but linked, houselike buildings. The project exemplifies the concept of accommodating multiple smaller units in a community of large houses set within a garden. The goal of the design was to promote a sense of community and a townscape for a population that includes households of single parents, unrelated individuals, and multigenerational families.

Program and site design

The resident population at La Brea Franklin was considered too large—if kept as an undifferentiated group—to get to know each other, share facilities, and ensure the safety and maintenance of the complex. In response, the project is organized around several smaller environments with a clear hierarchy of public and private spaces. Four courtyards step down to the east, following the natural slope of the site, to allow light into the courtyards and to provide views from the upper levels of the units. Approximately 10 households share one common courtyard and covered porch, which serves both as a shady gathering place overlooking

▷ *View of La Brea Franklin Family Housing in Los Angeles. Ten houselike buildings in a garden setting actually contain 40 dwelling units. Photo by David Hewitt/Anne Garrison; © David Hewitt/Anne Garrison.*

the garden and as a rainy-day play area. Curved shapes and contrasting colors give architectural emphasis to this semipublic space. Ramps connect the different levels of the courtyards, and diagonal views open the courtyards in two directions.

The project includes numerous places designed to encourage neighbors to socialize, children to play, and plants to flourish. A collective environment that supports the residential life of a group of families is the emphasis at La Brea Franklin. The development is large enough to allow a mix of users and small enough to allow mutual support systems to develop. Each houselike grouping is made up of a representative cross-section of households.

▲ The original competition model for the La Brea project shows the courtyard concept and the separate buildings. The Santos Prescott and Associates project won a Los Angeles Museum of Contemporary Art competition for prototype housing. Photo by Squidds & Nunns.

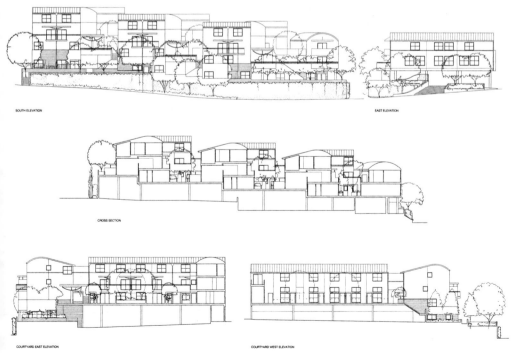

SOUTH ELEVATION

EAST ELEVATION

CROSS SECTION

COURTYARD EAST ELEVATION

COURTYARD WEST ELEVATION

◀ Section shows the parking deck with courtyards and building above. Each level of the deck has a separate vehicular entry from the sloping alley to the side of the project. Santos Prescott and Associates.

▶ *Section shows how units step down the hill for access to sun and views. Santos Prescott and Associates.*

The courtyards step down to the east, following the natural slope of the site.

Parking

The deck on which the buildings and court-yards are built hides 73 parking spaces for the development. Automobile access to the project is confined to an alley, both to conceal the cars from passersby and to avoid increasing traffic on busy Franklin and La Brea avenues.

Building design and construction

To optimize light conditions, the buildings are lower in scale to the south and the east. Each unit has two exposures for light and air, and all kitchens are day-lit. The two-, three-, and four-bedroom units are all

▶ *Each 10-unit group shares a semiprivate porch. It serves as a shady overlook to the garden and a place for children to play on rainy days. Photo by David Hewitt/Anne Garrison; © David Hewitt/Anne Garrison.*

Each courtyard has a community porch that provides a shady spot from which to overlook the garden.

townhouses with open plans and country kitchens that overlook a living area. Views at both ends of living spaces and lofts in the second-level units give them a spacious feeling.

Every unit has an individual entry and private outdoor space. Several units have bedroom suites with a separate entry from the deck level, giving these spaces the flexibility to be used as home offices or separate living quarters. By careful stacking of units and by locating unit entries on opposite sides, the plan gives each multilevel unit multiple outdoor spaces and two entries.

Each cluster of households shares a garage and a laundry and lounge area as well as a play space and a covered porch. All

◀ *View of a typical courtyard with a path and plants. Photo by David Hewitt/Anne Garrison; © David Hewitt/Anne Garrison.*

▼ *The La Brea Franklin site plan shows the courtyards and other gathering spaces for smaller communities of 10 households each. Santos Prescott and Associates.*

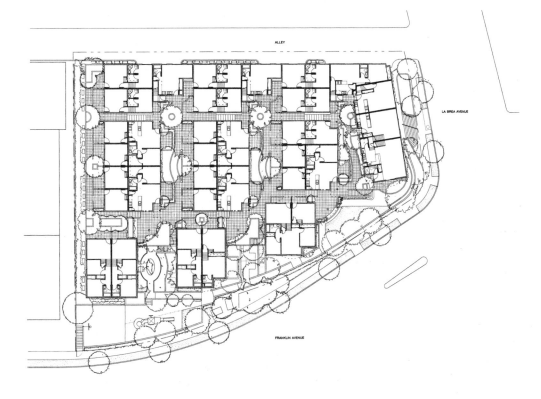

The living room on the entry level looks into the entry garden, while the kitchen/dining space overlooks the living room and has a small private patio.

▶ *Kitchen overlooking living area in a unit at the La Brea Franklin complex. The dwelling units have open plans with cross-views, level changes, and private outdoor space. Photo by David Hewitt/Anne Garrison; © David Hewitt/Anne Garrison.*

community facilities—the community room, the laundry room, and the parking—are located on the ground level and are fully accessible to people in wheelchairs.

The buildings are clad in stucco, with standing-seam metal roofs and painted steel rails and trim. The distinctive curved roofs of the project were designed to provide headroom on mezzanines while keeping courtyard walls as low as possible. The project is built with conventional wood framing, which allowed for the greatest flexibility in planning. The garage deck comprises post-

tensioned concrete slab supported on concrete columns and concrete masonry unit (CMU) walls.

LA BREA FRANKLIN FAMILY HOUSING, Los Angeles, California

Owner / Developer: Thomas Safran and Associates

Master planner: Santos Prescott and Associates

Architects:

Design architect: Santos Prescott and Associates

Executive architect: Carde Ten Architects

Contractor: Campbell Construction

Key consultant: Structural engineers: Kurily Syzmanski Tchirkow

Project description: Urban, multifamily housing with integrated parking. Courtyard access to houselike units that range in size from studio to four-bedroom, three-story units. All units have private outdoor space and two orientations for light and ventilation.

Completion date: Competition, 1988; constructed, 1995

Number of units / type / size:

2 studios, 500 sq ft

10 one-bedroom, 650 sq ft

15 two-bedroom. 800 sq ft

8 three-bedroom 1,100 sq ft

5 four-bedroom, 1,300 sq ft

40 units 30,600 sq ft

Site size: 33,000 sq ft

Density: Approximately 53 units per acre

Parking: 73 spaces in two garages under building (40 direct-access, full-size spaces; 33 compact, tandem spaces)

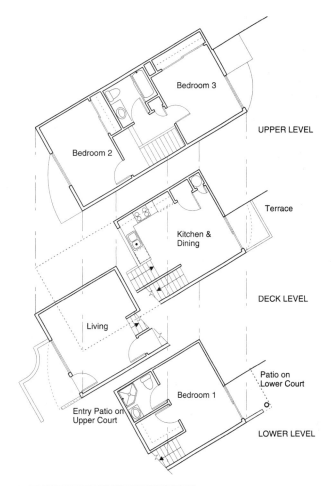

UPPER LEVEL

Bedroom 3

Bedroom 2

Terrace

Kitchen & Dining

DECK LEVEL

Living

Patio on Lower Court

Entry Patio on Upper Court

Bedroom 1

LOWER LEVEL

◄▲ Cross-section of a typical two- or three-bedroom townhouse in the La Brea Franklin complex. The separate-entry suite at the lowest level provides flexibility. Santos Prescott and Associates.

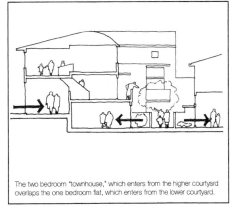

The two bedroom "townhouse," which enters from the higher courtyard overlaps the one bedroom flat, which enters from the lower courtyard.

CHAPTER 4

THE ROW HOUSE AND OTHER LOW-RISE HOUSING

From the courtyard houses of ancient Ostia and Athens to contemporary planned communities, townhouses are a basic building block of city life. (The terms townhouse, terrace housing, and row house are used interchangeably throughout this book.) Characterized by relatively narrow and deep proportions, with front and back windows and often fireproof party walls on each side (or small gaps between houses as in San Francisco, for example), townhouses are usually built in rows with similar floor plans and some exterior visual relationship to each other. Ranging from one to five stories in height, townhouses may house one family or several families. They allow for private entries to individual dwelling units within a narrow width of street frontage, thus minimizing the length of utility runs and providing for high-density, low-rise dwellings of, generally, 25–40 units per acre in a townhouse neighborhood.

Townhouses are an efficient, flexible, and livable solution for families, and they may also be attractive to singles and empty nesters who do not want to be burdened

◀ A townhouse neighborhood in Richmond, Virginia. Photo by Jean Lawrence.

Plate 52.

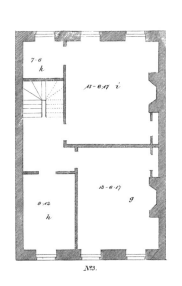

with the greater upkeep of a freestanding house. Townhouses aid the successful transition from less to more dense housing types in mixed-type housing communities, and they are as well adaptable to urban, suburban, and rural areas (rural townhouses are less common but not unusual in resort or other clustered developments). Built tightly together, townhouses make efficient use of land, allowing higher densities and preserving outdoor space. Shared party-wall construction conserves materials and reduces energy requirements for heating and cooling. In addition, some of the most walkable and attractive city streetscapes in the United States and abroad are townhouse neighborhoods in, for example, London, San Francisco, Amsterdam, Boston, and Richmond, Virginia.

BACKGROUND

The American row house is most directly related to English prototypes and has evolved over the past 350 years. By the time of the growth of cities in the American Colonies, townhouses were commonly developed in groups with similar layouts. Guiding builders were pattern books of designs such as Asher Benjamin's *American Builder's Companion* (1806).

Regional variations came about as a result of differences in climate, local culture, building code requirements, and topography. Over time, many cities enacted requirements for fire-resistant construction—often in the wake of catastrophic fires. Initially, the open space behind row houses was needed for privies and stables, but developments in building systems now allow this space to serve as gardens or parking.

One impetus to townhouse construction in this century has been the movement to-

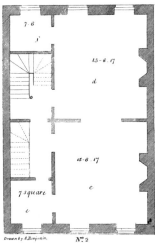

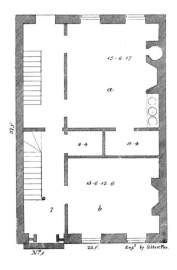

▲ Illustration of a townhouse from Asher Benjamin's American Builder's Companion (1806). The layout of townhouses has changed little since that era. Reprinted from Dover Publications.

ward denser cluster developments to preserve open space. Another is the acknowledgement that row housing may be a more promising prototype for urban family life than high-rise buildings, especially for lower-income families. Row house units sell or rent at more affordable prices than detached houses, and they require less maintenance because they use less land and have fewer exposed surfaces (which also results in more efficient use of energy for heating and cooling). An emphasis on planned new communities in Germany in the 1920s spurred investigation of and experimentation with housing types by Bauhaus architects and others, and this continued through the twentieth century in Germany and elsewhere. Experiments in neighborhood design and the increased scale of construction led to more comprehensive neighborhood planning, where attached houses conformed to one another in style and were built in batches by private developers.

Note that current building codes in the United States are often more stringent than older codes or those of other countries in terms of fire egress, for example. Older or foreign building prototypes may require substantial variations to meet today's requirements for new buildings, although buildings erected prior to the codes may be able to continue in use under some code provisions.

THE BASIC BUILDING TYPE

Because windows are limited to the front and back of the building and it is efficient to keep the units relatively narrow to increase density with less street frontage, the interior unit designs of townhouses are fairly limited and consistent. Units are generally at least 15–16 ft wide and can be 30–90 ft in depth. Wider houses (over about 18 ft) effi-

ciently allow space for two bedrooms side by side on both exterior walls, to create a four-bedroom unit on two levels. Deeper row houses yield relatively large areas in the middle without light; light wells, skylights, or courtyards can sometimes provide natural light for these areas (these devices are feasible in one-story row houses or in wider, multistory buildings). Generally, however, the habitable rooms occupy the window walls at the front and back of the building, with utility spaces (stairs, bathrooms, kitchens, mechanical space, and closets) grouped in the middle.

To vary dwelling-unit size within the same basic module in houses along a row, some units can step up and down or forward and back with minor modifications of the typical design. Although the basic townhouse concept does not lend itself well to handicapped access, accessible units may be created within a row of multistory townhouses by forming a double-wide unit at grade in the width of two townhouse modules or expanding an end unit outward

▲ *Modernist low-rise housing in Munich, Germany, incorporates child care and office space in its lower floors. It also establishes a flexible framework for building additional floors at the top and for personalizing the basic structure. Steidle + Partner. Photo by Michael Joyce.*

▶ *A typical townhouse plan. Although dimensions and details may vary, the basic layout provides a practical arrangement of rooms in a limited-width building.*

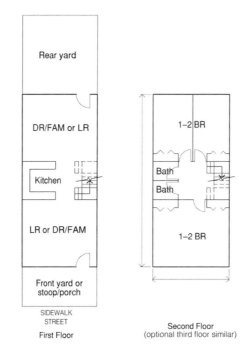

Rear yard

DR/FAM or LR

Kitchen

LR or DR/FAM

Front yard or stoop/porch

SIDEWALK
STREET

First Floor

1–2 BR

Bath

Bath

1–2 BR

Second Floor
(optional third floor similar)

▼ *Longitudinal section through a row of two- and three-story townhouses showing the range of dwelling unit types that can be accommodated within the module.*

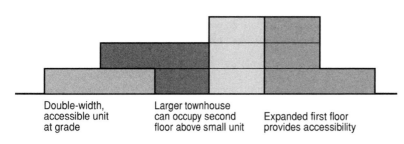

Double-width, accessible unit at grade

Larger townhouse can occupy second floor above small unit

Expanded first floor provides accessibility

to incorporate more space at grade level. Row houses may be entered at grade, a half-level above or below, or a full story above grade, with equal variety possible at the back of the unit. Depending on natural slopes and unit designs, this can provide for many variations in design and use.

Cultural and individual differences combine to determine a family's preference about public/private and formal/informal uses of space. It may be possible (and desir-

able) to provide individual flexibility, even within a standard unit layout. For example, the townhouses at Harbor Point, Boston, are designed so that the front and rear first-floor rooms can be used interchangeably as a dining and family room or formal living room. Each family chooses which room they want to face the back yard and which to face the street. When combined with variations in relation to grade, virtually endless options may be achieved by the creative use of interior space. These include such possibilities as incorporating an apartment or workspace on the ground level or moving living areas to the top of the building to take advantage of views, light, or higher ceilings.

SITE DESIGN AND PARKING

Townhouses generally sit quite close to the street, often with a small front garden and a stoop or front porch to create a comfortable, semiprivate zone between street and dwelling. The density in row house communities has the advantage of providing enough foot traffic to create pedestrian activity and safety along the street as well as opportunities for meeting neighbors.

As with most housing, accommodating cars can be a defining challenge in site design; a number of different approaches are possible. Parallel parking in front accommodates, at most, one car per townhouse width and is the least intrusive way to park. It allows for the space behind townhouses to be used as private or shared yards. Parking at 90 degrees to the curb along one or both sides of the street increases the number of cars that can be accommodated but widens the street and may detract from its character. Parking can also be aggregated in small lots near the housing. With more than one car per family now common, particularly as

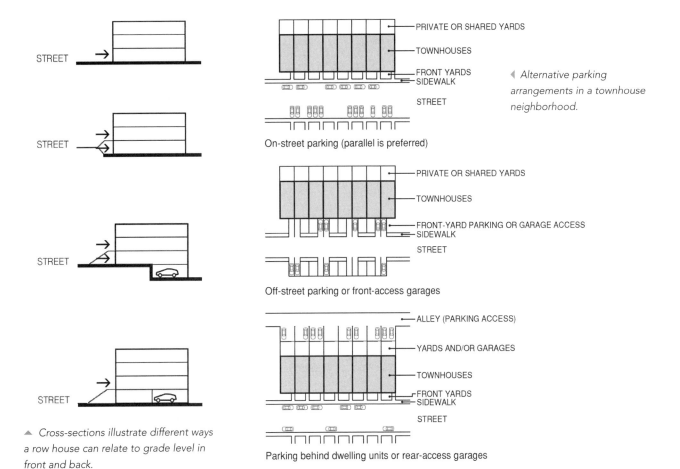

STREET

STREET

STREET

STREET

▲ Cross-sections illustrate different ways a row house can relate to grade level in front and back.

PRIVATE OR SHARED YARDS
TOWNHOUSES
FRONT YARDS
SIDEWALK
STREET

◀ Alternative parking arrangements in a townhouse neighborhood.

On-street parking (parallel is preferred)

PRIVATE OR SHARED YARDS
TOWNHOUSES
FRONT-YARD PARKING OR GARAGE ACCESS
SIDEWALK
STREET

Off-street parking or front-access garages

ALLEY (PARKING ACCESS)
YARDS AND/OR GARAGES
TOWNHOUSES
FRONT YARDS
SIDEWALK
STREET

Parking behind dwelling units or rear-access garages

townhouses become an increasingly popular suburban housing prototype in the United States, either the zoning or the market may require off-street parking for each dwelling. However, green rating systems such as Leadership in Energy and Environmental Design (LEED) create incentives to reduce or eliminate parking if local zoning doesn't require it and if public transit is available.

A parking garage that occupies the front of the house at grade level or somewhat below grade, leaving space for an entry to one side, is one way to provide off-street parking. This configuration has the disadvantage of frequently interrupting the sidewalk with driveways and creates a less direct relationship between the house and the street. Alternatively, parking can be located behind row houses, with an alley for access. This has the advantage of providing service access to the houses (for trash pickup, etc.) but decreases private outdoor space and security in back of the houses; it may also decrease activity (and the safety it can bring) in the front of

▶ Section showing structured parking below row houses at Langham Court, Boston. Goody Clancy.

the houses. Another approach is viable only when land values justify the cost of structured parking: townhouses and their patios can be built atop below-grade parking garages, effectively hiding the parking while freeing the grade-level site for other uses (see Langham Court case study, p. 83).

VARIATIONS

The row house's long history and its flexibility have led to many variations: the same basic unit type has yielded everything from modest two-story workers' townhouses to

▶ Townhouse units can be combined with flats in taller buildings.

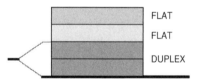

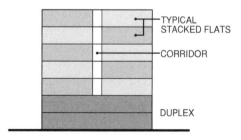

lavish urban palaces. As cities have grown and land values have risen, increasing housing density has been a goal that has made the ideal dwelling unit tall and narrow. The need for greater housing density has led to the conversion of many of the grand townhouses originally intended for single families into multiple dwelling units.

A number of variations are possible for combining townhouse-style units with other unit types. Stacking townhouses vertically is another way to accommodate more dwellings while retaining some of the character of a single-family house and the convenience and pleasure of direct access to the outside. A key design requirement under most modern building codes is the provision of two separate egress stairs from any unit that lacks direct access to grade. The upper townhouse may be located anywhere from one-and-a-half to three levels above grade (still in the walk-up range); by grouping four units around two egress stairs, the need for two independent means of egress can be met economically (see the floor plans for Langham Court, p. 88). Townhouses may also occupy the base of any taller building (called maisonettes) with flats above. This arrangement mixes housing and family types in one building, and the multiple entrances and privately maintained yards may enliven the ground level.

◀ Row houses in Hastings, England, show the great variety that can be achieved in two- and three-story row houses of a consistent width. Photo by Ian Britton/Freefoto.

▼ A row of contemporary townhouses detailed in steel and glass, Wohnbebauung Jugerhalde, Germany, shows a successful high-tech vocabulary. Project and photo by Schaudt Architekten.

Creating new townhouse units in the many deteriorating and obsolete three-story buildings of flats built as public housing in the mid-twentieth century has also given new life to communities. This kind of conversion reduces the number and sizes of the families that share a common entry, thereby increasing security, and assigns the use and maintenance of adjacent exterior space to each row house unit.

EXTERIOR DESIGN

In the selection of materials, detail, and window placement, the facade of a townhouse row should maintain a balance between consistency and individuality, simplicity and visual interest. The facades may be sheathed in wood, brick, stucco, metal, stone, concrete, or a combination of materials. Although austere identical elevations can be beautiful, variation of detail from one house to the next may give houses individuality within a

▲ Greenwich at Garfield Place, a multifamily rental apartment building, also incorporates retail uses. This 148-unit building was the first of six phases planned for a new residential neighborhood in downtown Cincinnati, Ohio. Project and photo by Gruzen Samton LLP, Architects Planners & Interior Designers.

related vocabulary. Variation in height or minor shifts forward or back can create a livelier rhythm in a long row of houses, as can smaller-scaled elements such as entryways, balconies, or bay windows. Roof forms can run the gamut of pitched to mansard to flat.

Attempts to copy exactly nonlocal or historic architectural styles generally look artificial and out of place. Although historic recall may be a very successful design tool, it must be exercised with skill, subtlety, and restraint to be successful. Contemporary design can use new building materials and techniques to achieve a high-tech aesthetic; this aesthetic is more common for housing developments in Europe than in the United States.

OTHER LOW-RISE HOUSING

The definition of low-rise buildings in the
United States used to reflect the number of
stories occupants are willing to climb, above
which an elevator is needed. However, current building code requirements in this country generally change for buildings taller than
three stories, and the Americans with Disabilities Act (ADA) requires elevators in all new
multifamily buildings over one story or otherwise not accessible by wheelchair. In this
book we consider buildings up to four stories
(with or without an elevator) to be low-rise.

Multifamily low-rise buildings (as opposed to the townhouse-style buildings discussed earlier in this chapter) are typically
built today as flats, with apartment sizes
ranging from studios to two-bedroom units.

Garden apartment buildings cluster four
or more dwelling unit entries on each floor
around a circulation core, minimizing corridors. This building type is characterized by a
single street entry serving a small number of
dwelling units; it is often a freestanding
building (with open space on four sides).
Older-style garden apartment buildings,
with one means of egress and no elevator,
cannot be built today in most localities; few
new garden apartments are likely to be built
in the United States because of the high cost
of providing an elevator for so few units.

More typically, low-rise multifamily
buildings have a single central entry with interior corridors that can extend as far as
building codes and market preferences allow,
with egress stairs located to provide two independent means of egress from every unit.
The unit types and building configurations
possible are similar to mid-rise buildings de-
scribed in the next chapter. The elevators are
generally centrally located.

GARDEN APARTMENTS

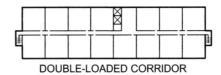

DOUBLE-LOADED CORRIDOR

SINGLE-LOADED CORRIDOR

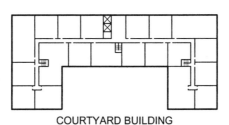

COURTYARD BUILDING

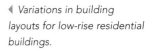

◀ *Variations in building
layouts for low-rise residential
buildings.*

CASE STUDIES

Borneo Sporenburg
Amsterdam, Netherlands

Confined to two connected peninsulas in the Eastern Harbor Docklands of Amsterdam, Netherlands, the plan for Borneo Sporenburg confronted the planning challenges of a dense urban environment. The planners had to achieve a balance of public and private zones within a small area, and the surrounding water represented both an opportunity and a limitation—a public realm for the community but also a boundary. The plan for Borneo Sporenburg set a density of 100 units per hectare (41 units per acre) as a requirement, and ultimately

2,500 units were built. The plan incorporates a number of building types; but the reliance on townhouses provides the required density and creates a vital and cohesive community.

Planning and site design
The two peninsulas of Borneo and Sporenburg, located at the eastern end of the Amsterdam docks, are tied together by twin bridges that cross a wide basin. The bridges accommodate cyclists and pedestrians, connect neighborhoods to one another, and focus attention on the basin itself, the backdrop of the development. The public domain of Borneo Sporenburg is the water, a unique characteristic of canal communities.

▷ *An aerial view of the Eastern Docklands shows the development of the Borneo Sporenburg site. Photo by Jeroen Mulsch.*

◀ Two sister bridges connect Borneo and Sporenburg. The higher pedestrian bridge offers a glimpse into the secluded world of the patios. Photo by Jeroen Mulsch.

A variant of the traditional Dutch canal house, the housing at Borneo Sporenburg forms a *Scheepstimmer-manstraat*, a broad avenue of row houses lining the canal.

The overall site design emphasizes the interplay of built architecture and void. A diagonal green strip and two squares form a wide, open path that relates to the water. Street and quay design elements at Borneo Sporenburg are kept simple and consistent. Brick paving and oversized concrete curb stones are used for the straight and narrow streets.

Public sidewalks line the water's edge, but most exterior spaces, including patios and open spaces within the townhouse units, are the residents' private domain. The patios create sunlit voids within the densely built rows of townhouses. Glimpsed from the streets and the canals, they establish an interplay of public and private views.

◀ The variety in houses and boats enlivens the scenery at Borneo Sporenburg. Photo by Jeroen Mulsch.

▲ The townhouse facades' diverse architectural styles provide opportunity for individual expression while maintaining a consistent scale. Photo by © Archives West 8, urban design and landscape architecture.

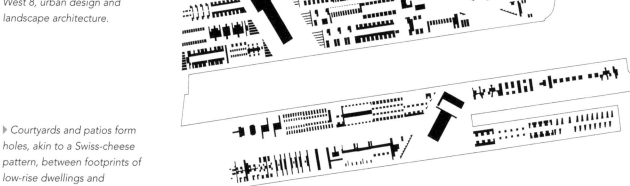

▶ Courtyards and patios form holes, akin to a Swiss-cheese pattern, between footprints of low-rise dwellings and sculptural blocks. West 8.

◀ *Patios within typical row houses at Borneo Sporenburg become private gardens. Photo by Jeroen Mulsch.*

▼ *The prototype dwelling at Borneo Sporenburg is defined by a 30–50 percent void with a private parking area. West 8.*

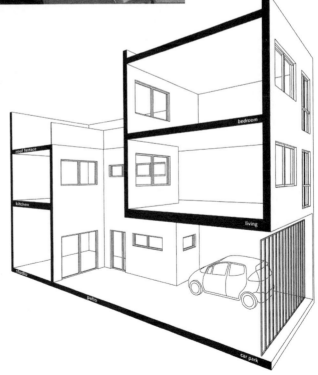

The existing quay structures were fully renovated. A floating museum ship called the Armada of Amsterdam added to the revitalization of the nineteenth-century docks. Such harborside activity reinforces the concept that "green is replaced by blue," that water is the dominant public space.

Building design

The Borneo Sporenburg dwelling was created as a prototype: a home with an attached garage and a 30–50 percent interior void. Five basic building types and a wide spectrum of floor plans were developed by different architects based on this prototype. While maintaining a consistent scale, diverse architectural detail lends individuality to the facades of the row houses.

The patios at Borneo Sporenburg—most of them visible from the streets and quays through glass facades—give residents an opportunity for individual expression yet pro-

▶ *View inside a Masten-broek and van Gameren house. A glass-enclosed patio offers the sensation of flying above the water. Photo by Jeroen Mulsch.*

▼ *Not only do the patios create private spaces for Borneo Sporenburg residents, they also provide interior light for the dwellings, illuminating units up to 15 m (45 ft) deep. Photo by Jeroen Mulsch.*

vide privacy in this dense urban community. Their small scale and individuality provide a welcome contrast to the open harbor landscape.

The townhouses are a contemporary equivalent of the traditional canal house, with taller living rooms facing the water. Greater living room heights are not only a desirable feature for the living units but also provide long-term flexibility, allowing future conversion of ground-floor units into retail, restaurant, and office space.

Set amidst the townhouses, three large sculptural blocks of apartments provide an opportunity for metropolitan apartment living and help vary the scale within the development. The variety of living options allows for a more diverse range of ages and social habits in the resident population.

Development process

The planning of Borneo Sporenburg was experimental and attracted great interest on the part of urban planning professionals and national planning authorities. During the intensive and participatory planning process, which included workshops, more than 100 architects contributed to both the urban plan and development of the housing prototype.

Large tracts of land in the Netherlands have traditionally been sold to developers who build housing and then offer it to individuals for resale. At Borneo Sporenburg, 60 parcels of undeveloped land were offered for individual ownership through a municipal lottery (called "free parcels"). This allowed the individual owners to exert a greater influence over the design of their houses and the development of the community. Workshops were held to guide owners and their architects in designing the row houses.

This individual ownership of land and design-construction by the owner has become a prototype in Dutch urban planning: free parcels are now integrated into most new planned neighborhoods in the Netherlands.

▲ Patios and open voids allow water and sky to meet, as expressed in this house by architect Koen van Velzen. Photo by Jeroen Mulsch.

BORNEO SPORENBURG,
Amsterdam, Netherlands
Owner / Developer: New Deal
Master planner: Integral urban design by
West 8/Adriaan Geuze
Architects: Over 100 different architects for
the free parcels, including: de Architecten-
groep, Koen van Velsen, and Inbo Archi-
tecten
Sculptural Apartment blocks:
  de Architecten Cie: "The Whale"
  Koen van Velsen: "PacMan"
  Steven Holl (original design) and Kees
  Christaanse (construction drawings and
  construction management): "The Foun-
  tainhead"
Key consultant: Ingenieursbureau
Amsterdam
Project description: Integral, low-rise, high-
density urban design, incorporating mid-rise
structural blocks and low-rise row houses.

Completion date: 1996–1997
Number of units / type / size:
  Total: 2,500 dwellings, sizes vary up to
  400 sq m (4,305.6 sq ft)
  "The Fountainhead": 150 dwellings and
  business spaces
  "PacMan": 204 dwellings and business
  spaces
  "The Whale": 214 apartments and busi-
  ness spaces
  Approximately 1,950 individual low-rise
  dwellings
Site size:
  Borneo: 13.1 hectare (32.4 acres)
  Sporenburg: 10.3 hectare (25.4 acres)
Density: 100 dwellings per hectare (41 per
acre)
Parking: One parking space per house; park-
ing types include the individual carpark, the
inner parallel street (inside the block), and
the half-sunken parking garage

Langham Court
Boston, Massachusetts

Langham Court is an urban residential complex with 84 units of housing in the heart of Boston's South End historic district. The development provides mixed-income housing in a variety of unit types, ranging from studios to three-bedroom duplexes, in buildings that fit the historic neighborhood. The design makes no distinction among its residents (one-third low-income, one-third moderate-income, and one-third market-rate)—all units are distributed equally throughout the complex. Although the development also includes a five-story mid-rise building housing flats, this case study focuses on the four-story townhouses.

▼ The courtyard at Langham Court. Open on the south side, the courtyard allows sun into the dwelling units and provides shared open space and private patios. Photo by Steve Rosenthal; © Steve Rosenthal.

▶ *Townhouses along the side streets have front stoops and bay windows. At the far corner, a tower element of the five-story mid-rise building is visible. Photo by Steve Rosenthal; © Steve Rosenthal.*

Site plan

The project occupies most of a city block, with the buildings wrapping around the perimeter on three sides and addressing the streets with narrow planted buffers and front stoops. Wide, two-story vaulted entrance-ways welcome the neighborhood into the south-facing, landscaped courtyard in the middle of the block. The open side of the courtyard faces an existing elderly housing complex across an alley, completing the quadrangle of buildings.

The garden court provides both semiprivate rear patios for the first-floor units and larger public terraces, seating areas, and lawns. The housing is constructed atop a below-grade parking structure, which is con-cealed from the street and courtyard. Parking ramps enter and exit the garage from the alley.

Building design

The townhouses are located on the side streets and reflect the Victorian character and smaller scale of the surrounding neighborhood. The design of Langham Court reinterprets some of the best features of the nearby historic buildings: dormers, bay windows, arched entryways, string courses, and varying roof forms (pitched, mansard, and flat). Materials include two colors of brick, granite, precast concrete, enameled aluminum, wood, and glazed ceramic tile. This vocabulary is integrated with restraint, con-

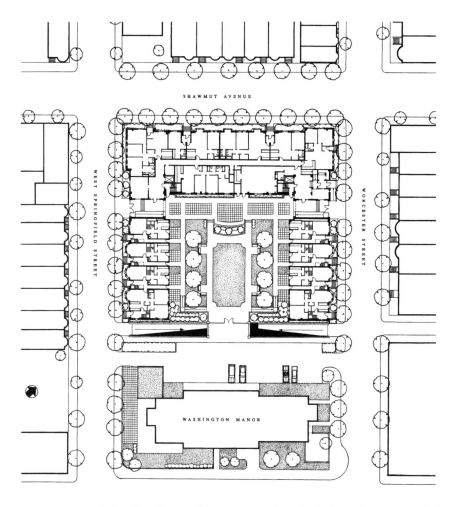

SHAWMUT AVENUE

WEST SPRINGFIELD STREET

WORCESTER STREET

WASHINGTON MANOR

◁ *Site plan of Langham Court. Townhouses and mid-rise housing surround the open courtyard (middle), with private patios for townhouse units on either side. The new housing matches the scale and relationships to the street of the existing neighborhood, with a mid-rise building on the major street (top) and townhouses on the side streets. Existing elderly housing is shown at the bottom of the drawing. Goody Clancy.*

tributing richness and detail to the simple building masses.

By stacking duplex over duplex, the townhouse design increases density while housing families in dwelling units that retain the intimacy, scale, and convenience of the traditional townhouse neighborhood.

Four townhouse units share two egress stairs located between them; each townhouse unit also has an internal stair. Because the first floors are a half-story above grade, the occupants of the upper units have only one-and-a-half flights of stairs to reach their private entrances. Raised stoops serve multiple purposes: they recall neighboring buildings, create a friendly urban gesture, and obscure the parking below.

Construction system

The structural system is a fireproofed, steel frame clad in a brick veneer. Although other structural systems might have been more economical if the entire project were townhouses, the steel system was selected as a

85

▶ *View through the archway into the courtyard. Townhouses are visible in the background and mid-rise units are located on the right. Photo by Steve Rosenthal; © Steve Rosenthal.*

contractor's recommendation to simplify construction by using one structural system for the townhouses, mid-rise buildings, and parking structure.

Financing and development

Langham Court was developed by the Four Corners Development Corporation, a non-profit community development group.

WEST SPRINGFIELD   COURTYARD   WORCESTER STREET

▲ Section through townhouses and courtyard showing underground parking. Goody Clancy.

◀ Detail of arch at Langham Court. Careful detailing gives the buildings a texture and complexity similar to the surrounding Victorian buildings but in a modern vocabulary. Photo by Steve Rosenthal; © Steve Rosenthal.

▶ *Plan of stacked three-bedroom duplex unit (typical upper unit shown). The two stairs between units provide the required two separate means of egress from each unit. Goody Clancy.*

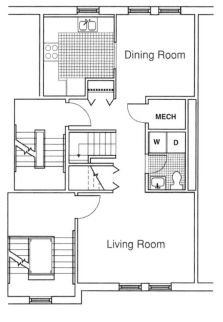

LOWER LEVEL PLAN

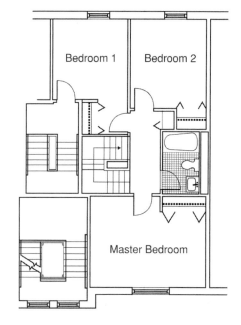

UPPER LEVEL PLAN

Comprising housing activists from the South End of Boston, the Four Corners Development Corporation (aided by the Boston Redevelopment Authority) launched the project. The group's goal was to make the complex aesthetically suited to its historic neighborhood and to house residents of mixed income levels. Langham Court was financed by city funds, state loans, and private investment, much of which was spurred by federal tax incentives.

LANGHAM COURT Boston, Massachusetts
Owner / Developer: Four Corners Development Corporation

Planner / Architect: Goody, Clancy and Associates, Inc.
Contractor: Dimeo Construction Co.
Key consultants:
    Structural: Lim Consultants
    Landscape: The Halvorson Co.
Project description: Urban mixed-income, mixed-type housing
Completion date: 1991
Number of units: 84 units total, 48 of which are within townhouses
Site size: 1 acre
Density: 84 units per acre
Parking: Underground parking for 54 cars

BedZED, A New English Garden City
Beddington, United Kingdom

The Beddington Zero Energy Development (BedZED) demonstrates how an environmentally responsible residential community can reconcile density with amenity, minimize its impact on the natural environment, and increase its residents' quality of life. Setting sustainability as a priority, BedZED was developed to reduce emissions expenditure and take advantage of natural resources within a community setting. The "green" lifestyle demonstrated at BedZED is so easy and convenient that most residents have slipped into it unconsciously.

Site design
Constructed on a site once used for waste treatment, BedZED houses a dense grouping

▼ An aerial view from the southeast of the development depicts the interplay of built and open space at BedZED. Bill Dunster Architects ZEDfactory Ltd. Photo by Raf Makda/VIEW.

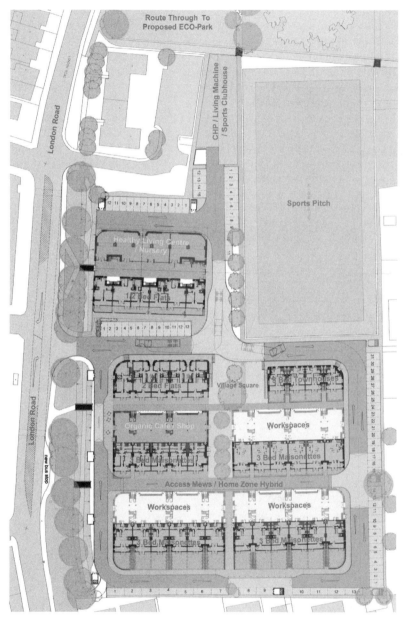

Site plan. The mixed-use development consists of dwellings, live-work units, a community center, and a nursery. By locating housing near amenities, the development's plan significantly reduces residents' ecological footprint. Bill Dunster Architects ZEDfactory Ltd.

of solar-powered townhouses, most with their own roof garden and southern-facing conservatory. Located outside of Sutton, England, BedZED is an easy commute from London, yet many residents work within the community. The mixed-use development includes workspace, an office park, day care, and athletic facilities. Although densely built, it offers more amenities than most suburban communities.

Building innovations and design

BedZED generates enough heat and power from renewable resources to make it nearly carbon neutral. Energy is provided by several means, including a combined heat and power unit fueled by woodchips from the development's own trees. Photovoltaic panels and tilted skylight units generate solar energy; wind-driven heat-recovery ventilation units take the place of electric fans; and photovoltaic cells charge shared electric cars. All of these elements, along with sedum-covered roofs and grass-covered terraces (providing insulation), contribute to BedZED's playful design. These innovations and variations in design have created a community that is diverse in use, building materials, and unit type.

BedZED's loftlike row houses are built primarily with local, recycled, or reclaimed materials. The 82 maisonettes and 18 live-work units combine brick, gypsum plasterboard, concrete aggregate, and topsoil. Exterior carpentry and bridges were built with Forest Stewardship Council–certified hardwood, and reclaimed steel has been brightly painted to add a modern touch to an otherwise traditional building type. Despite relatively small floor plans, sunlit conservatories and gardens give the townhouses a spacious feel.

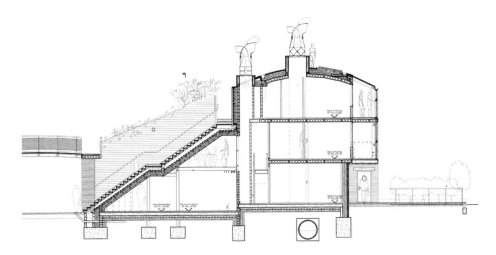

◀ The buildings are aerodynamically designed for natural ventilation. The shape also allows for sky gardens and preserves solar access for neighboring buildings on the north. Bill Dunster Architects ZEDfactory Ltd.

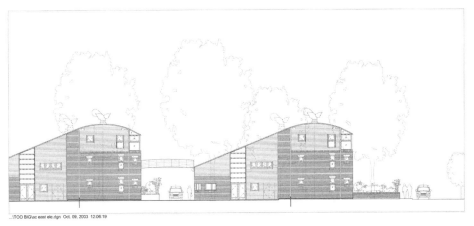

...\TOO BIG\ac east ele.dgn Oct. 09, 2003 12:06:19

◀ This east elevation of the development depicts the connection of one unit to another. Bill Dunster Architects ZEDfactory Ltd.

Development

This ambitious approach to "green design" has been beneficial to the developer and buyers alike. Putting environmental design aside, the comfort level, affordability, and convenience of BedZED's mixed-use, live-work environment, three-level townhouses, and proximity to the local train station have made BedZED an attractive investment. BedZED was built by an eco-minded developer in partnership with a charitable housing association dedicated to producing environmentally and socially sustainable homes.

BedZED established legal precedents as the first project to be allowed zoning advantages in exchange for lower environmental impacts. This precedent makes new carbon-neutral, mixed-use developments attractive to developers as well. Although the initial capital cost may be higher for environmentally focused developments, the expense is quickly offset by a reduction in operating costs.

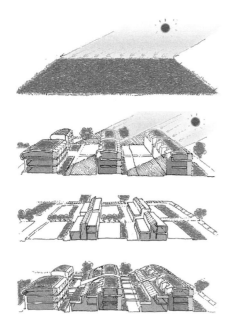

▲ Each solar-oriented block is strategically placed to avoid overshadowing the block behind it. Placing live-work units on the north of the blocks leaves each dwelling with a garden. Revenue from the gardens pays for the development's green technologies. Bill Dunster Architects ZEDfactory Ltd.

▶ This computer-generated image shows a range of units at BedZED. Sky gardens are accessed by bridges from the dwellings opposite. Bill Dunster Architects ZEDfactory Ltd.

▲ Live-work units contribute to the high level of daytime activity at BedZed. Bill Dunster Architects ZEDfactory Ltd. Photo by Raf Makda; © Raf Makda.

BedZED, A NEW ENGLISH GARDEN CITY, Beddington, United Kingdom
Owner / Developer: Bioregional Development Group/Peabody Trust
Master planner / Architect: Bill Dunster Architects ZEDfactory Ltd.
Contractor: Gardiner and Theobald CM
Key consultants:
    Mechanical and electrical: ARUP
    Structural: Ellis and Moore
    Quantity surveying: Gardiner and Theobald CM

Project description: Mixed-use, solar-powered urban development
Completion date: 2002
Number of units / type: 100 low-rise attached units
Site size: 1.7 hectares (4.2 acres)
Density per acre: 59 units per hectare (24 units per acre)
Parking: 82 spaces, and a car club that houses two cars shared by the development's residents

▲ This view of the homes on the south of the site shows photovoltaic cells in the sun space and ground-floor gardens. Bill Dunster Architects ZEDfactory Ltd. Photo by Raf Makda; © Raf Makda.

CHAPTER 5

THE MID-RISE

BACKGROUND

Until the late nineteenth century, multifamily urban housing was limited in height by the maximum number of flights of stairs occupants could reasonably be expected to climb to reach their apartments—hence the four- and five-story row houses, low-rise buildings, and garden apartments discussed in Chapter 4. Occasional six- and seven-story walk-ups were developed to achieve the highest possible density on valuable sites in fast-growing urban areas, but these housing types are no longer built in the United States.

In the mid-nineteenth century, the introduction of the passenger elevator as a reliable and affordable means of vertical transportation forever changed height constraints for all building types. Although office buildings were the first to use elevators to increase density and create multistory buildings as image and status symbols, the housing industry soon followed suit.

Early mid-rise housing in larger cities was often built around courtyards; the resulting U- or E-shaped footprints produced the longest perimeter possible on the site while ensuring daylight for interior rooms. These configurations were built to the greatest height the market or, later, zoning allowed. Architects dealt with the formal design issues of taller residential buildings in much the same way as they did with the higher commercial buildings that preceded them: expressing a base, a shaft, and a top in a range of styles. These early mid-rise buildings were built to the street edge, continuing the fabric of the traditional city around them but at a far greater density.

THE BASIC BUILDING TYPE

Mid-rise housing, as we have defined it for the purposes of this book, is an aggregation of dwelling units in buildings ranging from approximately 5 to 15 stories. These buildings require elevator access, but they are

▼ The Regatta, a waterfront mid-rise building at Battery Park City, New York City. Gruzen Samton LLP, Architects Planners & Interior Designers.

▶ *Typical double-loaded and single-loaded building layouts.*

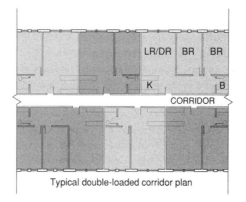

Typical double-loaded corridor plan

Typical single-loaded corridor plan

▼ *Typical one-bedroom unit plan with window exposure on one side.*

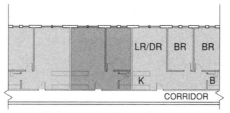

SERVICE FUNCTIONS (NO DAYLIGHT)

LIVING ROOMS (DAYLIGHT)

generally broader than they are high. The mid-rise housing discussed in this chapter consists of lower, broader, horizontal building masses as opposed to the higher tower forms discussed in Chapter 6.

Flats in these building configurations may be organized along a single-loaded corridor (a row of flats opening off one side of the corridor) or a double-loaded corridor (a row of flats opening off both sides of the corridor).

The double-loaded approach is more efficient in terms of circulation space; but single-loaded schemes are appropriate where an exterior access corridor is feasible, where views make one side of a building more desirable, where a site is narrow, or where the units wrap around another structure such as a parking garage. Whether a building plan is single- or double-loaded, elevators generally will be centrally located, with egress stairs at the corridor ends.

Whether single- or double-loaded, the units created typically have only one exterior exposure. An interior zone that parallels the corridor is used for entry, circulation, kitchen, bathrooms, and storage. An exterior zone, with its windows, is reserved for living and dining areas, bedrooms, and a possible study.

Units at the building's ends, corners, and setbacks can take advantage of multiple exposures. Balconies related to living and dining areas, whether recessed into the building mass or projecting from it, are a desirable feature.

Mid-rise housing of six and seven stories is common in urban and suburban areas. A reason for this can be found in the generalized groupings of allowable maximum building heights common under zoning ordinances and bylaws. Beyond the row house and low-rise category, the first common zoning height limitation is 60–75 ft, which corresponds to six or seven stories. Although zoning height restrictions increasingly reflect more complex formulas involving multiples of density, setback distances, and facade lengths, many older maximum-height limits still prevail. Equally important are building codes. For example, the International Building Code (IBC) states, in the high-rise category, that all buildings with an occupied floor above 75 ft require access for fire department vehicles.

There are additional reasons for mid-rise construction. High-rise towers have steeper construction costs (for structural reasons), and thus are generally suited for more expensive markets where land is more valuable. Mid-rise buildings can provide a large number of units at a feasible cost, and they can also present an active street-level facade (through direct-access ground-level units) and promote a stronger sense of community.

SITE DESIGN AND PARKING

Mid-rise housing may be shaped to reinforce the street line in an urban context, defining both the public exterior space and private courtyards (in the center of the block) for residents. This approach suggests parking within a structure (i.e., structured parking) that is ideally below grade but possibly in an adjacent building, which may cost less.

Another urban approach to mid-rise site design wraps single-loaded units around an above-grade parking garage for the first few stories, creating a shared outdoor space on the garage roof that is open to residents.

In a suburban location, or one where land is less valuable, surface parking may be the only economically feasible approach. Good site design is critical to avoid surrounding the mid-rise building with a sea of cars.

Topography and surroundings may suggest ways to organize (or subdivide) a building's parking to minimize its impact. For the drop-off of visitors and for residents coming from parked cars, building entries must relate to the direction of approach. Good landscaping and lighting improve the appearance of parking lots.

Local zoning rules define minimum parking requirements, but location, income

▲ A mid-rise building steps down to make the transition from downtown to a smaller neighborhood scale. Tent City, Boston, Massachusetts. Goody Clancy. Photo by Steve Rosenthal; © Steve Rosenthal.

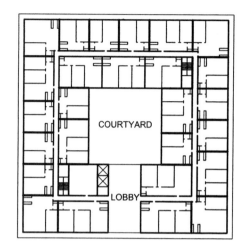

▶ *Diagram of a building that continues the line of the street and creates a private courtyard in the middle of the block of apartments.*

▶▶ *Surface parking building options: a preferred and a less desirable alternative approach to the design of surface parking.*

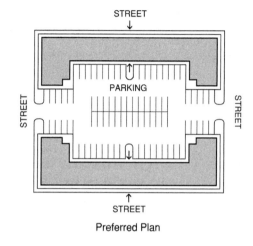

Preferred Plan

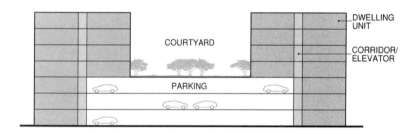

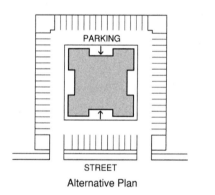

Alternative Plan

▲ *Section showing dwelling units that wrap around a parking structure to take advantage of exterior exposures, hide parking, and create a more attractive street edge. A courtyard over parking can create attractive outdoor space and allow daylight into dwelling units on either side.*

mix, and access to public transportation are equally important in influencing the number of parking spaces necessary. While parking requirements for low- and moderate-income housing normally vary from 0.75 to 1.5 spaces per unit, depending upon location and income mix, market-rate housing may require two or more spaces per unit. In addition to the spaces dedicated to residential units, visitor parking must be accommodated.

VARIATIONS IN BUILDING PLANS

Skip-stop plans locate a corridor only on every second or third floor. Units are two stories and are entered from the corridor, with internal stairs leading to the unit's second level (either above or below).

The primary advantages of skip-stop planning are that it allows exposure on both sides of the building for one floor of each unit; development of a partial two-story living area within the unit; and less area devoted to corridors. The primary disadvantage is the area required for internal stairs in every apartment.

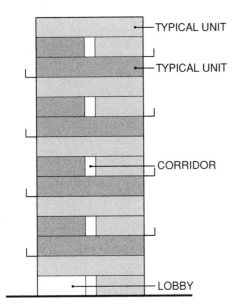

TYPICAL UNIT

TYPICAL UNIT

CORRIDOR

LOBBY

◀ Section showing the skip-stop elevator concept.

▼ Loft units provide spacious living areas or live-work units for a certain market, for example, 1310 East Union, Seattle, Washington. Miller/Hull-David Miller. Photo by James F. Housel.

ferent types of housing with direct access from the street or for uses other than housing, such as retail or office space. (See Chapter 1 and the tables in Chapter 2, p. 18-20 for more on mixed-type and mixed-use development.)

BUILDING AMENITIES AND SERVICES

Amenities and services provided in mid-rise buildings vary greatly depending upon the

In addition to the conventional apartment and through-floor layouts, lofts may be used in any of the configurations discussed above. Artists seeking low-cost, spacious accommodations with high ceilings and large windows for use as live-in art studios first developed loft-style apartments in rehabilitated industrial or warehouse buildings. Ceiling heights (up to 20 ft) and large industrial windows provide the space and quality of daylight that artists seek. Loft plans typically create a mezzanine or inter-floor level along the rear or corridor wall. Sleeping areas (lofts) on the upper level are open to the studio space below, whereas entry, kitchen, and bath functions occupy the primary floor beneath the mezzanine. Loft living has become so popular with nonartists that new residential buildings are being built to resemble old lofts, even in areas where there is no historical loft precedent.

The first (and sometimes second) floor in a mid-rise (or high-rise) may be used for dif-

size of the building, the income mix, and the building ownership or leasing structure. Basic front-of-house facilities may include an entrance lobby, front desk, elevator core, management office, and some form of mail-and-package delivery system. Back-of-house facilities may include a security center, service entrance, loading dock, freight (and moving day) elevator, trash-removal system (possibly including an area with dumpsters, compactors, and recycling facilities), tenant storage areas, and mechanical, electrical, and building maintenance facilities. Luxury buildings, whether rental units or condominiums, often provide additional tenant amenities such as more generous lobbies, concierges, lounges, meeting rooms, health clubs, pools, and other indoor or outdoor recreational facilities.

EXTERIOR TREATMENT

This discussion of mid-rise housing focuses on lower, more horizontal building masses rather than slender towerlike forms. The exterior appearance of mid-rise housing is influenced by the overall building configuration, the structural system, and enclosing wall materials, as well as the presence of balconies, roof terraces, or sun-control devices. The overall building mass may range from the simplest boxlike volume to more complex forms with varying roof levels and projecting wings enclosing courtyards or defining shared exterior spaces.

Expression of Structure

A concrete frame may be exposed as an integral exterior design element. A steel structure, however, must be fireproofed and clad in a finish material if it is to be expressed on the building's exterior. Due to its expense, this gesture is rarely made. Generally, the structural system of a residential building is not treated as a design element on the exterior but is buried within the exterior walls.

Exterior Wall Materials

The building's enclosing wall material, or its skin, is one of the most prominent aspects of its appearance. The skin combines two systems: an opaque material and a transparent fixed or operable window system. (Since this discussion applies both to mid-rise and high-rise buildings, the illustrations show examples of both building types.)

The most common opaque exterior wall material is brick. Historically, brick walls were often load-bearing walls, built of thick masonry and incorporating stone sills and lintels. Contemporary brick walls, however, are usually constructed as a single wythe of brick veneer supported by a metal-frame backing to which the brick is attached or tied. This construction system is lighter in weight and allows space within the wall for moisture drainage as well as for the installation of air- and moisture-infiltration barriers and thermal insulation. Other masonry materials, such as concrete block and glazed ceramic or terra-cotta tile, are sometimes used for exterior wall finishing,.

Stone has also traditionally been used as a durable exterior wall material. As with brick, it originally took the form of thick load-bearing walls incorporating stone lintels, sills, and accessories and later evolved into a thin veneer applied over a metal-framed backing system.

Precast concrete wall panels are another common exterior wall enclosure material. They may be supported on or hung from a steel or concrete frame, and they typically span vertically, from floor to floor. Precast concrete is often used as a complete exterior

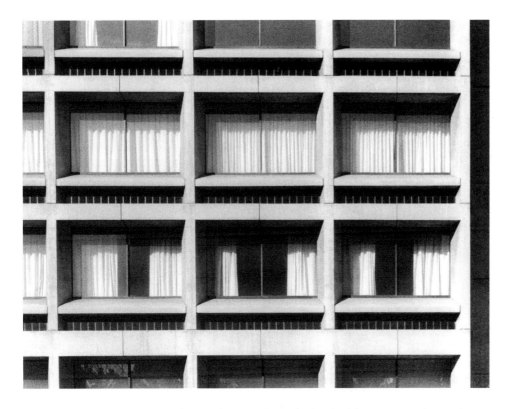

◀ An example of meticulous concrete detailing at University Plaza, New York City. Although this example is a high-rise, the project illustrates how concrete can be used as an architectural element. Pei Cobb Freed and Partners. Photo by George Cserna.

enclosure system that includes facings for exposed structural elements, window frames, and other exterior items.

Buildings may also be built completely of cast-in-place concrete, including the structure, enclosing walls, and other miscellaneous exterior elements. Outstanding examples of architectural concrete include much of the architecture of I. M. Pei. Architectural concrete requires extensive on-site labor and is therefore generally not competitive in today's market. Far less expensive is a stucco finish; however, the synthetic stucco (exterior insulation and finish system, or EIFS) widely used in the past had technical problems as well as a much coarser appearance than traditional stucco. Contemporary systems can be designed to be made drainable, which helps

limit the kind of deterioration that undermined earlier systems in certain climates. Even these refined systems, however, are less durable than concrete or stone, and more vulnerable to damage from physical impacts.

Window Openings

Window units in multifamily buildings consist generally of two types: a "punched" opening in a solid wall with a sill 30–36 in. above the floor (for flexibility in furniture placement) is most often used as a bedroom window, while a large glazed area, sometimes reaching from floor to ceiling, may be used in living and dining areas. Glazed areas may open onto a balcony or terrace that may either project from the wall or be recessed into the building mass.

▶ *The design of interior unit plans is reflected in the elevations of 100 Memorial Drive, built in the late 1940s in Cambridge, Massachusetts. Stacked plans create large-scale vertical elements (left); a skip-stop configuration is reflected in two-story volumes (right). Ralph Rapson et al. Photo: Goody Clancy.*

Efficient multi-unit planning groups dwelling units in pairs. These units should be organized with back-to-back baths and kitchens that share vertical mechanical and electrical chases, with identical units stacked one above the other. This type of plan establishes noticeable, large-scale, repeating vertical patterns along the building facade. For example, stacked, identical two-bedroom units in a building translate visually into approximately 50-foot-wide vertical bands of solid wall with punched window openings alternating with an approximately 44-foot-wide vertical band of glass window wall with possible projected or recessed balconies. This overall patterning creates strong vertical elements that accentuate the height of both mid-rise and high-rise buildings (as shown on this page).

Window Walls

Exterior metal grid-wall systems, commonly called window wall or curtain wall systems, typically comprise a nonstructural metal grid attached to the structure and infilled with a combination of fixed glass panels, an operable sash, and opaque glass or metal panels. Opaque panels may be made with a composite of materials, including the necessary exterior skin, moisture barrier, thermal insulation, and interior finish. Although steel and aluminum windows and window and curtain walls are available, anodized or prefinished aluminum is a more commonly used material. Most of the discussion about exterior wall materials and window composition for mid-rise residential buildings applies equally to high-rise housing, which is addressed in Chapter 6.

CASE STUDIES

Yerba Buena Lofts
San Francisco, California

The Yerba Buena Lofts are spacious dwellings set within a dense urban center. Through local incentives, the Lofts were designed to take maximum advantage of height allotment, building up to 85 ft, after setting aside 10 percent of the units for affordable housing. Although the building appears from the street to be 5 stories, it is actually a 10-story structure composed of double-height residential units. The expression of the double-height units, indicated by terraces and bays, creates a lively elevation of alternating open and enclosed spaces. The high ceilings give residents additional freedom to shape their own space rather than being restricted by a programmed floor area.

Site
The Yerba Buena Lofts are located in San Francisco's South of Market (SoMa) district, between Fourth and Fifth streets and fronting Folsom and Shipley streets. The project has 200 units of loft-style residences and includes parking and ground-floor commercial space. The project's large scale and contemporary design of repetitive bays befits SoMa's urban fabric of old industrial buildings without mimicking their design.

Taking advantage of the city's setback requirements, the Lofts also incorporate private gardens for the ground-floor apartments.

◀ The Yerba Buena Lofts are located in San Francisco's South of Market district. The projections and voids of bay windows and balconies form an egg-crate pattern on the building's exterior. Stanley Saitowitz Offices/Natoma Architects, Inc. Photo by Tim Griffith.

THE MID-RISE

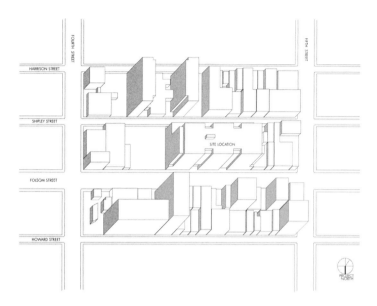

▲ Axonometric view of the Yerba Buena Lofts site. This drawing shows how the Lofts relate to the scale of the South of Market district's existing architecture. Stanley Saitowitz Office/Natoma Architects, Inc.

▶ Rhythmic placement of bays marks the Lofts' elevations and alludes to the area's existing architecture. Stanley Saitowitz Office/Natoma Architects, Inc. Photo by Tim Griffith.

▶ Ground-floor plan showing the structure of the building with a "lot," or structural bay, for each loft. The two street faces are lined with units that surround the parking. Units on the first four levels are entered directly from the parking area. Stanley Saitowitz Office/Natoma Architects, Inc.

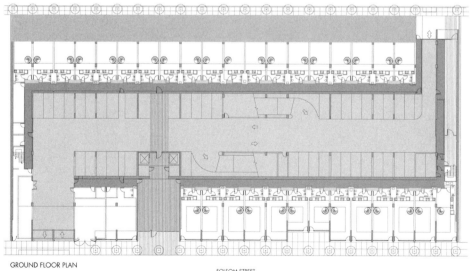

GROUND FLOOR PLAN

◀ *The Yerba Buena Lofts'
geometric glass-cube
projections create a complex
roof line. Stanley Saitowitz
Office/Natoma Architects, Inc.
Photo by Tim Griffith.*

Building design

The grid of the building's facade echoes San Francisco's street grid. The building's footprint is divided into distinct lots, each one housing a loft. The exterior of the building is referred to as an "egg crate," formed by the projections and voids of translucent glass bay windows and carved-out balconies. The bays and balconies are two stories high, reflecting the interior loft space. Glass cubes (windowed bays of the upper units) project above the roof, creating an articulated skyline of geometric peaks. Metal grating, in various patterns, forms guardrails for the

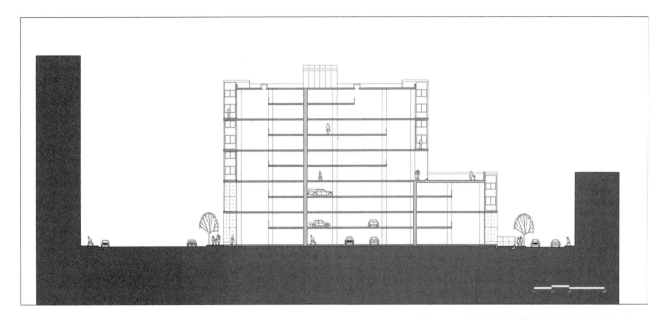

▲ Typical building section.
Stanley Saitowitz Office/
Natoma Architects, Inc.

▶ The exposed concrete
structural walls are a
dominant interior feature.
Stanley Saitowitz Office/
Natoma Architects, Inc.
Photo by Tim Griffith.

◀ The lofts have a mezzanine level, high ceilings, and ample daylight. Stanley Saitowitz Office/Natoma Architects, Inc. Photo by Tim Griffith.

balconies. This melding of materials, both familiar and new, integrates the South of Market industrial building type with San Francisco's traditional streetscapes.

Construction

The Lofts are composed of concrete load-bearing walls and post-tensioned concrete floors. The concrete serves as both a

LOWER LEVEL

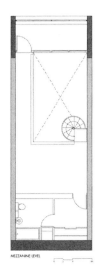

MEZZANINE LEVEL

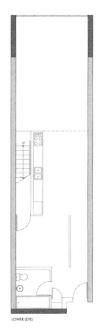

LOWER LEVEL

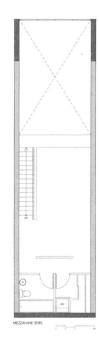

MEZZANINE LEVEL

▲ *Type three floor plan. There are five main unit types, each a two-story volume with a sleeping loft overlooking a common area. All units have a full wall of glass, a carved-out balcony, and a private exterior space. Stanley Saitowitz Office/Natoma Architects, Inc.*

▶ *Type two floor plan. Upper-level units have an additional sleeping area and full bath on both levels. Stanley Saitowitz Office/Natoma Architects,*

construction material and a finish, expressing the building's structure on both the interior and exterior. The concrete construction, used along with a system of "flying" forms for floors, allowed for fast and simple construction.

Parking
A four-level garage is embedded in the middle of the site. Residences on the lower four floors wrap around the garage, masking the structure from pedestrian view and providing same-level parking spots for the lower-floor lofts.

Unit design
Double-height units and private outdoor areas, provided by balconies and terraces, bring open space and daylight to each unit. This project shows that even in a dense area, loft design can provide spatial volume and flexibility for the urban dweller.

YERBA BUENA LOFTS,
San Francisco, California

Owner / Developer: Ed Tansev YBL LLC
Architect: Stanley Saitowitz Office/Natoma Architects, Inc.
Contractor: Pankow Residential Builders
Consultants:
Structural: Watry Design Group
Acoustical: Charles M Salter Associates
Project description: 200-unit residential loft building
Completion date: January 2002
Number of units / type / size:
200 units
5 basic types, each type 650–1,400 sq ft
Site size: 338' × 165' (55,770 sq ft or 1.4 acres)
Density: 143 units per acre
Parking: 200 cars

Colorado Court
Santa Monica, California

Colorado Court is one of the first housing projects in the United States to be designed to high standards of green construction; specifically, it was the first Leadership in Energy and Environmental Design (LEED®)–certified multifamily building in the United States, and it achieved a gold rating. The program consists of 44 single-resident-occupancy units, a community room, and a mail room, as well as shared courtyard spaces and parking.

This project represents an effort to help maintain socioeconomic diversity in a city with high housing costs and few afford-able options, as the units are affordable to low-income residents. The City of Santa Monica leased the land to the nonprofit developer at a long-term rate of $1 per year, and the city, the state, and regional green-building funding sources all contributed funding.

Because the development used several relatively new technologies, the architects had to work closely with building inspectors to clarify the intent of their design, as well as collaborate with the City of Santa Monica to get state energy-metering regulations changed. The completed building represents a successful public-private partnership, and it can also be studied as a model of sustainable development in an urban environment.

◀ The southwest facade of Colorado Court, Santa Monica, California, is the most highly articulated, with staggered towers supporting vertically oriented photovoltaic panels. Photo by Marvin Rand.

1 Lobby/Lounge
2 Common courtyard
3 Kitchen
4 Office
5 Entry
6 Storage room
7 Mail room
8 Laundry
9 Mechanical
10 Parking
11 Electrical room
12 Trash/recycling

▶ *The building is located near the on-ramp to a freeway, with access to public transportation, and within walking distance to many services. Pugh + Scarpa.*

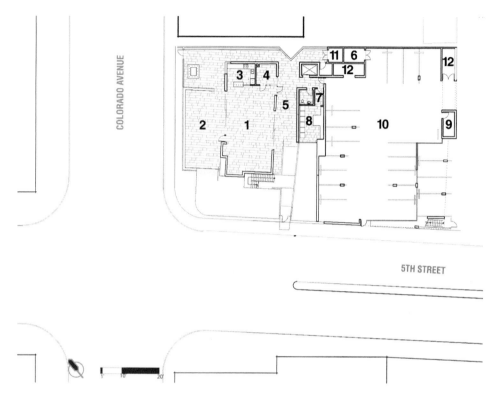

COLORADO AVENUE

5TH STREET

Site

Located in Southern California, the site receives abundant sunlight, and thus the building has a greater need for cooling than for heating. Colorado Court is oriented on its site to take maximum advantage of solar energy, daylighting, and prevailing winds. The solar panels face south, and windows are placed to promote cross-ventilation through every unit.

The project greatly exceeds local requirements for water reclamation. Colorado Court sits at a low point on the block, and its underground chamber system allows for capture of almost 100 percent of the entire block's storm-water run-off. The chambers release collected water slowly for reabsorp-

tion into the earth, where pollutants are filtered out by the soil.

The urban site, located near the on-ramp to a freeway, offers access to public transportation, and lies within walking distance of the beach and of downtown shopping and services. There is on-grade covered parking for 20 cars and a bicycle storage room on the ground floor.

Building design

Colorado Court is designed to be 100 percent energy-neutral. A highly visible sign of its technology is the integrated photovoltaic wall panel system. These solar panels generate power during the day and deliver any excess to the grid. They also shade the building.

The building is constructed of wood framing over a concrete base, with a stucco exterior.

Other exterior finishes are concrete masonry unit face block, recycled light-gauge steel, and galvanized sheet metal. The low-E windows are double glazed. Thermal, blown-in insulation made from recycled newspaper increases thermal resistance by 75 percent over a traditional wall.

The building is designed for passive cooling and shaped to induce buoyancy for natural ventilation. South-facing windows are shaded, and west-facing glazing is minimal to prevent afternoon and evening heat gain. North-facing windows allow prevailing breezes to enter the units. The ground- and second-floor levels incorporate shared outdoor courtyard spaces that act as "wind scoops" to increase ventilation. There is no mechanical air-conditioning system; instead, the prevailing winds provide thermal comfort.

▲ Different materials and colors are juxtaposed to create a unique design vocabulary, and layering creates a strong interplay of light and shadow. Each tower has exterior, single-loaded walkways that allow daylight and fresh air to reach the units. Photo by Marvin Rand.

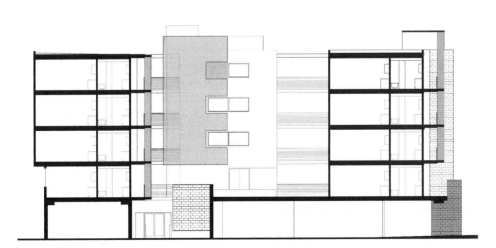

◀ Typical building section. Pugh + Scarpa.

▲ *The north elevation is punctuated by a pattern of small windows that capture prevailing breezes for interior ventilation. Photo by Marvin Rand.*

The solar panels were designed to supply about 30 percent of the building's electrical needs. A natural gas microturbine would supplement the panels, generating electricity and capturing its own waste heat to provide heat and hot water. Because the solar panels and microturbine would provide excess energy to the grid during the day and the building would draw energy from the grid as needed at night, the net draw of electrical from the grid was projected at zero. This required installation of a net-metering system to keep utility bills at zero, which state regulations originally prohibited—but the design team and the city's lobbyist worked with a state senator to change the regulations. The utility company then prohibited use of the microturbine, because its policy was to allow net metering only if the sole source of energy generation is solar or wind. As a result, the turbine has been turned off, and only the solar panels are being net metered.

Colorado Court is a fine example of the integration of sustainability—both passive and technological—into an affordable housing project.

COLORADO COURT,
Santa Monica, California
Owner / Developer: Community Corporation of Santa Monica
Architect: Pugh + Scarpa
Contractor: Ruiz Brothers, Inc.
Key consultants:
  Structural engineers: Youssef Associates
  Mechanical, electrical, and plumbing: Storms and Lowe
  Energy: Helios International, Inc.
Project description: Multi-unit affordable housing
Completion date: 2002
Project size: 30,150 sq ft
Number of units / type: 44 single-resident occupancy units of 300–375 sq ft
Site size: 15,000 sq ft
Parking: 20 on-grade parking spots

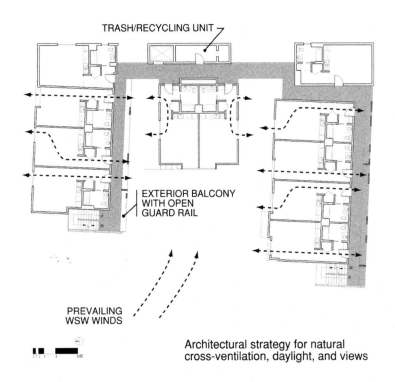

TRASH/RECYCLING UNIT

EXTERIOR BALCONY
WITH OPEN
GUARD RAIL

PREVAILING
WSW WINDS

Architectural strategy for natural
cross-ventilation, daylight, and views

◀ *Colorado Court is designed
to encourage natural
ventilation through all units,
with operable windows on
outer walls and operable
transoms above corridor
doors. Pugh + Scarpa.*

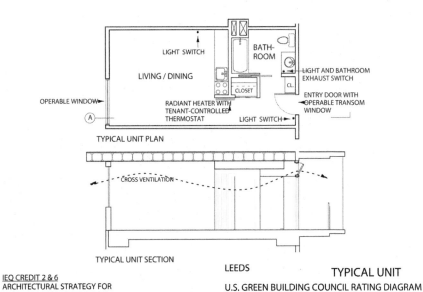

LIGHT SWITCH

BATH-
ROOM

LIVING / DINING

LIGHT AND BATHROOM
EXHAUST SWITCH

CLOSET

CL.

OPERABLE WINDOW

RADIANT HEATER WITH
TENANT-CONTROLLED
THERMOSTAT

ENTRY DOOR WITH
OPERABLE TRANSOM
WINDOW

LIGHT SWITCH

Ⓐ

TYPICAL UNIT PLAN

CROSS VENTILATION

TYPICAL UNIT SECTION

LEEDS

TYPICAL UNIT

U.S. GREEN BUILDING COUNCIL RATING DIAGRAM

PUGH SCARPA KODAMA 08.21.01

IEQ CREDIT 2 & 6
ARCHITECTURAL STRATEGY FOR
NATURAL CROSS VENTILATION.
CONTROLLABILITY OF SYSTEMS.

Tango
Malmo, Sweden

The Tango housing project began as a commission for a housing exposition cosponsored by the Swedish government and private developers. The site is a reclaimed waterfront brownfield on which the architects were challenged to create a model of sustainable housing design. The Tango project turned out to be technologically innovative, environmentally responsible, and architecturally dramatic.

Building and site design

The outer edge of Tango's U-shape form conforms to the block, and the inner edge consists of eight steel-and-glass towers defining a landscaped courtyard. Bedrooms wrap around the outer edge, while living rooms in the towers face the courtyard with projecting balconies and roofs. On the street side, textured white concrete with louverlike ribbing—oriented horizontally with occasional vertical interludes—provides a contemporary reinterpretation of board-and-batten construction. A rectangular grid rules the

▼ *Eight vibrantly colored steel-and-glass towers dance around a landscaped courtyard at Tango in Malmo, Sweden. Photo by Werner Huthmacher, Berlin.*

◀ Textured white concrete provides a more discreet street presence, but the towers can be glimpsed beyond the entrance, providing a hint of the development's inner vivacity. Photo by Werner Huthmacher, Berlin.

▼ Tango is located along a former industrial waterfront. Photo by Werner Huthmacher, Berlin.

composition, although window placement is staggered to enliven the facade. The interior courtyard towers are vibrantly colored and shift off the orthogonal plan, providing a lively contrast to the outer facades, and generating the name Tango, because they turn slightly, as if they were dancing.

The courtyard contains marsh vegetation, fed by recycled rainwater, to mimic the nearby Öresund sound. The low-maintenance vegetation introduces biodiversity to the site with plant species selected for an ability to clean pollutants from the soil, which was contaminated by previous industrial activity. Wooden boardwalks lead to the center island, which functions as a shared social space.

Sustainability

A wind turbine and 3,000 sq ft of rooftop photovoltaic panels give Tango complete energy self-sufficiency. The photovoltaic systems and turbine work together to contribute heating and electricity to both the building and the district; they are owned not by the building's owners but by the

115

▶ *Roofs are partially covered in solar panels and sedum. Balconies extend living space to the outdoors at Tango. Photo by Werner Huthmacher, Berlin.*

▼ *A typical kitchen in the Tango development. Photo by Ole Jais.*

district heating system. The windows are triple glazed, with a layer of trapped argon gas, to provide an R-value of 6.5, compared to 1.5–2 for typical double-paned glass. The windows have built-in ventilators to provide fresh air to each unit; they can be programmed to open at a threshold temperature to keep the unit cool. The roof, in areas not covered by the photovoltaic panels, is planted with sedum (a nod to traditional Scandinavian sod roofs), which helps to absorb runoff during heavy storms, mitigate the heat island effect, and replenish oxygen to the atmosphere.

Technology

One of the most innovative features of the housing complex is an integrated information technology system. An "intelligent wall" runs along the center line of the plan to accommodate wiring, fiber-optic cables, and mechanical services. The mechanical systems include underfloor hot water channels and heated ceiling panels and, as well, convectors to provide cooling in warm weather. The unit's system for controlling lighting, indoor climate, and security can be accessed either through an information technology (IT) cupboard or on a personal laptop through a private Internet-based interface. From any location where there is access to the Internet, a resident can open windows, lock or unlock doors, reserve a community room, or perform a number of other functions or tasks.

Tango has won many awards, and residents are willing to pay up to three times more per unit area to live there than they would for a conventional building.

▲ Typical unit plan. Moore Ruble Yudell Architects & Planners.

▲ A typical building floor plan shows the core "intelligent wall" as a bold line down the center. Bedrooms are aligned along the outer edge of the building, while living rooms project into the courtyard. Moore Ruble Yudell Architects & Planners.

◀ Typical section showing an upper unit and a lower unit. Moore Ruble Yudell Architects & Planners.

Section
1 Living room
2 Kitchen/Dining
3 Bedroom/Study
4 Loft/Library
5 Parking

TANGO, Malmö, Sweden
Client / Developer: MKB Fastighets AB
Design Architect: Moore Ruble Yudell
Architects & Planners with FFNS Architects
    Principal-in-Charge: James Mary
    O'Connor, AIA
    Executive Architect: SWECO Architects
    AB. Principal: Bertil Öhrström
Project Manager: SWECO Projektledning
AB
Contractor: Thage Anderssons Byggnads AB
Key consultants:
    Structural engineers: Skanska Teknik AB
    Mechanical, electrical, and plumbing: Pe-
    terson Göran VVS-Byrå AB, Hb2 VV

Steknik AB Magle Teknisk Service, Bengt
Dahlgren AB
Landscape: Moore Ruble Yudell
Architects & Planners and SWECO
Architects AB
Project description: Four-story market-rate
apartment housing block
Completion date: 2001
Project size: 46,528 sq ft
Number of units / type: 27 apartments of
600–1,950 sq ft; consisting of three duplex
units and 24 one-level units
Site size: Approximately one acre
Parking: 22 parking spaces in a nearby
garage

CHAPTER 6

THE HIGH-RISE

High-rise housing is an essentially urban form that can be built to densities of over 200 dwelling units per acre. Many building codes define any building taller than seven stories as a high-rise. For this book, however, we have classified *mid-rise* as multifamily housing between 5 and 15 stories (discussed in the previous chapter) and *high-rise* as buildings taller than 15 stories.

By concentrating the population needed to support a variety of retail, recreational, and cultural uses, the high-rise can help create vital districts as it has in cities like New York, Chicago, and Vancouver, British Columbia. Advances in performance-based seismic design have also led to the hitherto unprecedented construction of high-rises in earthquake-prone areas like San Francisco.

The high-rise can generate a level of pedestrian activity that encourages the informal interactions that help make these cities desirable places to live. Alternatively, though, when neither well-situated nor well-planned and when the difficult issues of parking and the building's relationship to the street are not successfully addressed, a high-rise building can interrupt the continuity of the city street and corrupt the quality of the surrounding urban life. High-rise housing is also increasingly built outside of traditional cities where spectacular views or some other amenity make a location valuable enough to support the costs of high-rise construction. Coastal areas in Florida and new suburbs with public transit to urban downtowns are examples.

◀ Skybridge, a new mixed-residential tower in Chicago with commercial uses at the base. Ralph Johnson, FAIA. Photo by Hedrich Blessing.

BACKGROUND

High-rise housing is a relatively recent phenomenon. The development of economical steel structural systems and efficient elevators in the late nineteenth century made the construction of higher buildings possible; the dramatic increase in demand for land in the urban cores of cities drove a trend toward placing dwelling units in higher buildings and changed the American urban landscape.

Housing construction, especially high-rise construction, virtually stopped with the Great Depression of the 1930s. It did not resume until after the Second World War. During this hiatus, the modern movement (and Le Corbusier, in particular) had developed a new philosophy and form for this building type: the housing tower in a park-like landscape, reflecting a preference for fresh air and good views over the virtues of dense, active streets.

The tall, slender tower was designed to accommodate the smaller family size that the postwar market required and, in keeping with the aesthetic of the modern movement, without a distinctive top or base to relate it to the ground. Economic pressure for cost-efficient building forms and new housing encouraged not only towers but also narrow, slab buildings, with dwelling units arranged on each side of a corridor and no limit to the length of the corridor or building. Neither of these efficient plan forms (unlike traditional urban housing forms) conformed to city blocks, and they were often built away from the street edge, in the middle of a block.

Government efforts to solve the housing problems of the urban poor with high-rise housing based on this model largely failed to create successful communities, especially for families with children. Typically, large and tall buildings in the shape of slabs or crosses (to maximize the perimeter) were set back from the street edge. They broke the traditional urban pattern of buildings that shaped the public street space and often substituted what became an unpopulated and unsafe no-man's-land between buildings. Families living on the upper floors were separated from the social activities of the street and from the play space for children below.

With a dramatic post–World War II increase in automobile ownership and denser residential construction in high-rise buildings, residents' cars could no longer be accommodated on streets. Cars were parked on the available site, around the buildings, turning "towers in the park" into towers in parking lots.

CONTEMPORARY HIGH-RISE HOUSING

Contemporary high-rise residential design has entered a period of unprecedented potential. For the first time, more than half of the world's population lives in cities. In some areas, demand for downtown office space has decreased, while demand for downtown living has seen an increase. Young professionals, baby boomers, and empty nesters often prefer city living, which is seen in a more positive light than it was a few decades ago. Mid- and high-rise living also appeals to many people, because it requires less time for maintenance, yard care, and so forth. High-rise buildings are an appropriate housing type in many circumstances. There are numerous examples of successful design, particularly for small and/or well-to-do families and on sites where views or other amenities make height an advantage. An upper-level unit with expansive views can be a status symbol and command higher prices. The greater density that results allows more people to live near the urban center, making it active around the clock.

An increasingly common and successful urban high-rise housing type combines commercial space and parking in a mixed-use building. This building type can both accommodate the large amount of parking required for projects of this size and integrate the smaller footprint of a housing tower with the larger traditional block pattern of the city. By building commercial space and parking within a broad, low base, the building can define the street edge and relate to lower buildings around it, while the housing rises in a slender tower above, independent of the street line. Placing retail uses on the street side of the base hides the parking structure and gives life to the street. (When the economics of the project permit it, parking can be below grade.)

Recent projects in New York, Boston, and Chicago are destination retail and entertainment centers, with a lively commercial character at the street level that serves as a base or plinth for housing that sits high above the noise and activity of the street and capitalizes on light and views. Some mixed-use high-rise towers include several floors of office space between the street-level retail and the housing above.

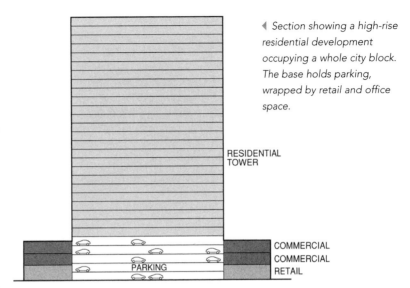

◀ Section showing a high-rise residential development occupying a whole city block. The base holds parking, wrapped by retail and office space.

RESIDENTIAL TOWER

COMMERCIAL
COMMERCIAL
RETAIL

PARKING

SITE DESIGN AND PARKING

Site Design

Site design strategies for high-rise housing vary with the surrounding context, but the best urban examples are organized on their site to relate to the urban pattern around them. Minimizing the negative environmen-tal impact of shadows, for example, is an important part of high-rise development planning. The shadows cast by a building on public spaces in and around the development site should be reviewed during design and may affect the building's form or orientation. Because wind accelerates around tall buildings, wind analysis is also a part of the design process for high-rise housing. These buildings should be designed to prevent excessive wind gusts at the entrance, the sidewalk, and at other public spaces around the building.

Parking

Parking is a crucial determinant of site design because a large amount of space is required to store residents' cars, even at lower urban parking ratios (the number of parking spaces per dwelling unit). Surface parking is the most economical in terms of construction cost but requires the most site area

121

▶ A 1960s "tower in a park" in Reston, Virginia, takes advantage of views and has a viable mixed-use community around it. Conklin Rossant. Photo by Dennis Swinford.

(approximately 350–400 gross sq ft per car). In areas where land costs are high enough to justify high-rise housing, those same costs may make surface parking prohibitive. Surface parking may also destroy the appearance of the site. Structured parking, either above grade or (where subsurface conditions permit) below grade, costs more to build but requires less site area. Often the building can be shaped to hide an above-grade garage from important street frontages. Below-grade parking has the highest construction costs but frees up the site for other uses.

Determining the required parking ratio is a step that must come early in the design process. Both zoning and market requirements will enter into this decision. The number of parking spaces required has a significant effect on site design options and the cost of the project. Locating large projects in areas well served by public transportation reduces the amount of parking required.

ARCHITECTURAL ISSUES

Elements of the Modern High-Rise

The entrance lobby at the main street-level entrance to the building makes the transition from the street and sidewalk (in some circumstances a vehicular drop-off area is provided) to the elevator core, generally located near the center of the building. The lobby is often the only public space of the building and will have mailboxes for residents nearby. In some buildings, additional community spaces (meeting rooms, function rooms, etc.) are provided at ground or roof level. If there is a parking garage, there may also be a separate entrance from the garage. Security is provided by building personnel, if there are any, or by an intercom or video system that allows residents to hear or see visitors before unlocking their doors.

High-cost housing may also have a security desk with a doorman or concierge in the lobby. The doorman or concierge provides services for residents—receiving packages, holding items for pick-up, etc.—and requires storage space nearby. High-cost high-rises may also provide in-building amenities for residents such as fitness centers, pools, and spas.

Similar lobby activities and spaces are appropriate for mid-rise buildings as well, but such space is better supported by high-rise buildings, because a single entry generally serves a greater number of dwellings. Although most apartment buildings have one at-grade, secure entry for all units, first-floor dwellings may have direct access to the street in what are sometimes called maisonettes. These units frequently serve as professional offices.

Two elevators is a typical minimum for high-rise buildings (allowing for one elevator to be out of service). More elevators are required in larger buildings, particularly when the building plan is extended laterally and when there is more than one entry. For example, in a full-block building there may be side-street entry lobbies and elevators as well. Separate service elevators are rare in today's market. See Chapter 8, "Building Systems," for more discussion of elevators in housing.

Two separated, fire-rated (typically within a two-hour-rated enclosure) and smokeproof stairs are the minimum required means of egress for each building. Building codes require that they be located as remotely as possible from one another (typically at or near the ends of corridors in slab buildings and at opposite ends of the elevator core in tower buildings). Codes generally limit dead-end corridors (the distance beyond the door to the egress stair at the end of the corridor) to 20 ft. The IBC allows 50 feet if the building is fully sprinklered. Designers must consult the applicable code for specific requirements. Scissor stairs, a pair of back-to-back straight-run stairs running in opposite directions, are acceptable in some code jurisdictions. They are often used in towers to save space.

After the destruction of the World Trade Center towers on September 11, 2001, more stringent safety requirements were introduced, including wider exit stairs, more storage capacity for sprinklers, and stronger fireproofing material. Updated versions of codes should be referenced to ensure that all code requirements are met.

Building Configurations

In a slab configuration, the dwelling units are arranged along a common corridor that leads to the elevator core (typically close to the center of the building). Egress stairs are required near the ends of the corridors. The simplest version of this form is a straight corridor lined by dwelling units and possibly with special larger units at the ends of the corridor. The building can bend into an L or a U shape to fit onto a particular site. In these configurations, building service functions (electric, telephone, and data closets, shafts, storage, or housekeeping) are usually located in the inside corners where there is no daylight.

A slab building can be double-loaded (with apartments on each side of the corridor) for the most efficient use of space, single-loaded (apartments on one side of the corridor only) to allow light into the corridor or to accommodate special site conditions, or a combination of the two. (See an example of double- and single-loading corridors in Chapter 5, p. 96.) In addition to code limitations, preferences of the intended residents of a building (the targeted market) will help determine the acceptable length of corridors within a building. Very long internal corridors may also result in a wall-like building form that is not aesthetically appealing from the outside.

In a tower configuration, the dwelling units generally surround a central elevator core, opening off either an elevator lobby at each floor or a circular corridor that wraps around the elevator core. The two egress

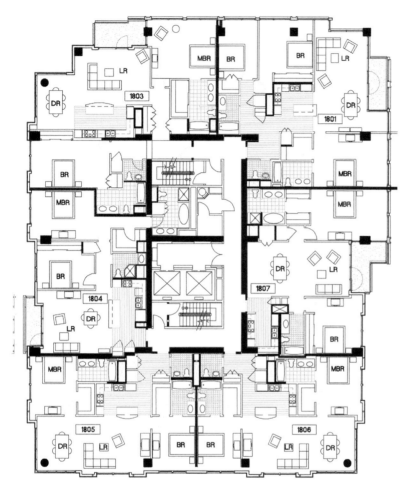

▲ Tower floor plans allow for a variety of unit designs, including four corner units per floor. Carrier Johnson Architects.

every other or every third floor. (For more discussion of skip-stop configurations and an example, see Chapter 5, pp. 98–99.)

Super High-Rise Buildings

The *super-high-rise,* or skyscraper, usually considered to be a building over 50 stories tall, was traditionally an office building type, but there are an increasing number of super high-rise projects that are primarily residential. Some have even been converted from existing office buildings. Very tall buildings must be braced against lateral wind loading on the upper levels, at minimum.

With advances in construction technology, high land costs, competition between regions, and a trend toward conspicuous consumption driving the luxury market, building height limits are being pushed ever higher. The ordinary skyscraper has been made to seem diminutive by the *super-sky-scraper,* loosely defined as over 1,000 ft tall, or about 80 stories and above. The city/state of Dubai, with several buildings existing or under construction that have been at one time designated "the world's tallest building," leads the world in the production of super-skyscrapers as a result of its large pools of available capital and low labor costs. Super-skyscraper construction has also seen a surge in several cities in the United States, such as Las Vegas.

Unit Types

High-rise dwelling units are similar to those in mid-rise buildings, with kitchen, bathrooms, and storage at the interior and living rooms, bedrooms, and sometimes dining rooms along the exterior. Because exterior exposure is at a premium, rooms are generally oriented with their shorter dimension at the window wall (see the typical unit layout, above left).

stairs, with their respective doors located as remotely as possible from each other, are located within the core. The tower plan in general offers more exterior exposures for the units (there is a higher percentage of two-exposure corner units) and greater flexibility in the layout of individual units than the slab plan. But because there are fewer units per floor (typically no more than eight), the building efficiency of the tower is lower than the slab.

Skip-stop configurations (with two-story dwelling units) require elevator stops only at

◀ The refined detailing of 860 Lakeshore Drive, Chicago, is a hallmark of Mies van der Rohe's International Style work. Photo courtesy Artifice, Inc./GreatBuildings.com.

The overall size of units varies with the income level of the residents they are designed to house and their location, but typical market-rate units are 600–800 net sq ft (NSF) for one-bedroom units; 900–1,200 NSF for two-bedroom units; and 1,100–1,500 NSF for three-bedroom units.[1]

High-rise buildings generally cater to single residents, couples, or small families in most parts of the country. Because of this, dwelling units larger than two bedrooms are uncommon except in luxury apartments or condominiums, which may include studies, dens, or libraries and will generally have larger rooms throughout.

Purchasing a unit in a high-rise condominium unit can be seen as a real estate investment. Even if investors do not reside in the unit themselves, they sometimes buy units to rent out and generate income.

Exterior Design

Because of their size and height, high-rise buildings have a presence both at street-level scale and, viewed from a distance, at the skyline scale. Their massing and detailing must address both scales. Early high-rise building designs were similar to their traditional antecedents: divided vertically into a street-level base; a middle level or shaft of varying height, depending on the size of the building; and a distinct top at the skyline. Window patterns, resulting from like units stacked one above the other for the sake of planning efficiency, were often composed on the building facade to emphasize height.

The modern movement broke with tradition by eliminating the expression of a building's base, middle, and top. Postwar residential high-rises were often composed as single, nearly undifferentiated shafts from

▶ Subtle handling of architectural details and the addition of balconies enliven a large brick facade near Berlin. Hans Kollhof and Arthur Ovaska. Photo by Michael Joyce.

ground to top. Some were refined objects with elegant surface treatment and subtle inflections at the top and bottom of the buildings, such as Mies van der Rohe's 860 Lakeshore Drive, Chicago. Other buildings of the modern movement were relentlessly bland and, with their lack of detail at the ground, were disengaged from the city around them. Examples of these are the public housing towers of the 1950s.

Well-designed contemporary high-rises may capitalize on the building's skyline presence by shaping an abstract top (perhaps containing elements of the building mechanical system or reflecting special housing units at the top floors) and integrating the

building into the life of the street at its lower levels. Often there are different uses, retail or commercial, at the ground floor that relate directly to the street (as shown on p. 121). This distinguishes the ground floor from the residential units that make up the body of the building above, creating a de facto base with an active, engaging edge where building meets sidewalk. Where retail is not appropriate, a different unit type (a flat oriented to the outside or a two-story townhouse type) can take advantage of the street frontage by opening to it with multiple individual unit entrances. In this model, these units may not be served by the buildings corridor system; they can be through-units, or they can wrap a parking structure (or other use that needs no frontage), hiding it from the street. For super-high-rise buildings, the building form often tapers as it rises, to allow for full-floor units toward the top with panoramic views.

Window units in multifamily buildings often consist of two window types: the bedroom window, with a sill located 30–36 in. above the floor for flexibility in furniture placement, and the larger living and dining area window, with glazing reaching to or near the floor. Because efficient multi-unit planning requires stacking paired, mirror-image units on multiple floors, the repetition of openings can create a large-scale pattern across the building's facade. The shape of window openings and the way they are combined may be used to emphasize the proportions of the building. Recently, there have been a number of all-glass facades with floor-to-ceiling windows in all rooms.

As with the mid-rise, numerous design devices are available to reinforce the patterns on the elevations that result from efficient

◀ *Balconies in a Berlin Seniorenwohnhaus contribute both visual richness and opportunities for meeting neighbors. Steidle + Partner. Photo by Michael Joyce.*

plan layout and stacking of dwelling units. Balconies, recessed terraces, and roof terraces add a level of visual richness to the building, a sense of human scale, and a framework for visible human activity on large buildings. Response to climate can distinguish parts of the building from one another and adapt the building to its location. For example, the use of sun-shading devices and the amount and shape of glass areas may vary with solar orientation. High-rise buildings today can also incorporate many other principles of sustainability, including building-integrated photovoltaics, geothermal heating, and their own wastewater treatment system (see Chapter 8 for more about building systems). One of the case studies for this chapter, Pelli Clarke Pelli's Visionaire building, offers a strong example of the incorporation of many sustainable features to achieve a high environmental rating, which is also marketable to potential residents. By their nature high- (and mid-) rise buildings are more sustainable, reducing the perimeter exposure of each unit to one or two walls and concentrating more people in a limited area to support public transit.

The building's enclosing wall material, or skin, is one of its most prominent features. It is a combination of an opaque wall material and a fixed or operable transparent window system. The most common opaque exterior wall material is brick, although many other materials are used, including glazed ceramic or terra-cotta tile, stone veneer, precast concrete, and metal panels. The discussion of exterior design in Chapter 4 (p. 73-74) also applies to high-rise buildings.

CASE STUDIES

Renaissance
San Diego, California

The west arrival plaza at Renaissance. These residential towers face a raised garden. Carrier Johnson Architects. Photo by David Hewitt/Anne Garrison.

Renaissance is a luxury condominium community in the Marina District of downtown San Diego, California.

The mixed-use complex includes multi-level retail, restaurants, lofts, townhouses, and flats. Two identical 22-story towers rise

above an elevated, terraced garden that conceals a four-level parking garage.

Renaissance is an important component in the redevelopment of San Diego's center city, which has had little residential population. Situated adjacent to Horton Plaza and near the historic Gas Lamp District, Renaissance is also convenient to other new civic and commercial developments that have reinforced the appeal of urban living in San Diego, where a grid is superimposed on the natural landscape of canyons and valleys. The relationship of topography and grid is a theme in the design of the project. The result is an "urban canyon"—a city block that is carved away by natural forms and elements.

Site design and parking
To provide adequate parking without building below the site's high water table, a partially above-grade garage was incorporated into the development. The desire to conceal the parking structure led to the concept of a walled garden. The walls run parallel to the street, conforming to the urban grid and providing street frontage for shops and residences. The organic forms of the terraced garden atop the parking structure contrast with the rigid city order. A grand, terraced stair connects the street to the elevated garden and main lobby of the buildings. The garden provides respite from the city below. Such amenities as barbecue grills and a swimming pool contribute to the feel of an informal neighborhood, as do lofts that open directly to the garden space.

Building design
The elevations of the towers reflect the different aspects of San Diego they face. The northwest elevations of each tower, which face the historic district, are sheathed in stone

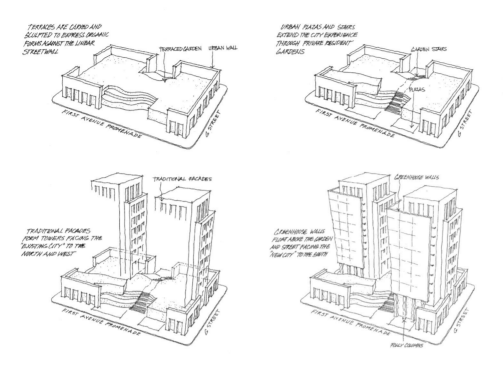

TERRACES ARE CARVED AND
SCULPTED TO EXPRESS ORGANIC
FORMS AGAINST THE LINEAR
STREETWALL

TERRACED GARDEN   URBAN WALL

FIRST AVENUE PROMENADE   G STREET

URBAN PLAZAS AND STAIRS
EXTEND THE CITY EXPERIENCE
THROUGH PRIVATE RESIDENT
GARDENS

GARDEN STAIRS

PLAZAS

FIRST AVENUE PROMENADE   G STREET

TRADITIONAL FACADES

TRADITIONAL FACADES
FORM TOWERS FACING THE
"EXISTING CITY" TO THE
NORTH AND WEST

FIRST AVENUE PROMENADE   G STREET

GREENHOUSE WALLS

GREENHOUSE WALLS
FLOAT ABOVE THE GARDEN
AND STREET FACING THE
"NEW CITY" TO THE SOUTH

FIRST AVENUE PROMENADE   G STREET

FOLLY COLUMNS

◀ These diagrams illustrate
the relationship between the
building elements and their
site. Carrier Johnson
Architects.

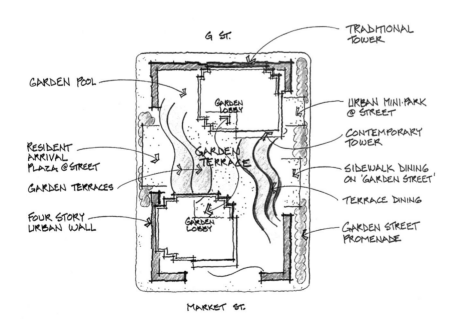

G ST.

TRADITIONAL
TOWER

GARDEN POOL

GARDEN
LOBBY

URBAN MINI-PARK
@ STREET

RESIDENT
ARRIVAL
PLAZA @ STREET

GARDEN
TERRACE

CONTEMPORARY
TOWER

SIDEWALK DINING
ON 'GARDEN STREET'

GARDEN TERRACES

TERRACE DINING

FOUR STORY
URBAN WALL

GARDEN
LOBBY

GARDEN STREET
PROMENADE

MARKET ST.

◀ A sketch of the site plan
of Renaissance provides an
overview of the site's mixed-
use components. Carrier
Johnson Architects.

▶ *This sketch of the building section illustrates how the garden terrace common area was created by berming the above-ground parking structure. Carrier Johnson Architects.*

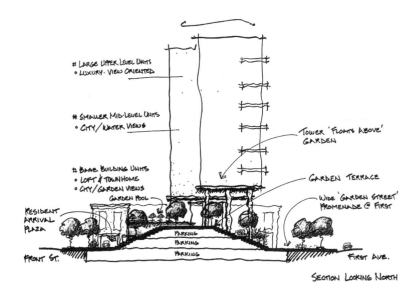

LARGE UPPER LEVEL UNITS
• LUXURY· VIEW ORIENTED

SMALLER MID·LEVEL UNITS
• CITY/WATER VIEWS

TOWER 'FLOATS ABOVE' GARDEN

GARDEN TERRACE

WIDE 'GARDEN STREET' PROMENADE @ FIRST

BASE BUILDING UNITS
• LOFT & TOWNHOME
• CITY/GARDEN VIEWS

GARDEN POOL

RESIDENT ARRIVAL PLAZA

PARKING
PARKING
PARKING

FRONT ST.

FIRST AVE.

SECTION LOOKING NORTH

▶ *A grand, terraced staircase draws residents of Renaissance up to the elevated gardens and garden-level lobby area. Carrier Johnson Architects. Photo by Anne Garrison.*

LOWER LEVEL
(LEVEL 3)

UPPER LEVEL
(LEVEL 4)

▲ The southeast facades of the twin Renaissance towers. The towers were designed to recall greenhouses. Carrier Johnson Architects. Photo by David Hewitt/Anne Garrison.

▼ A curving pathway leads past the townhouse entries. Carrier Johnson Architects. Photo by David Hewitt/Anne Garrison.

◀ Floor plans of a two-story townhouse that opens onto the garden-terrace level. Carrier Johnson Architects.

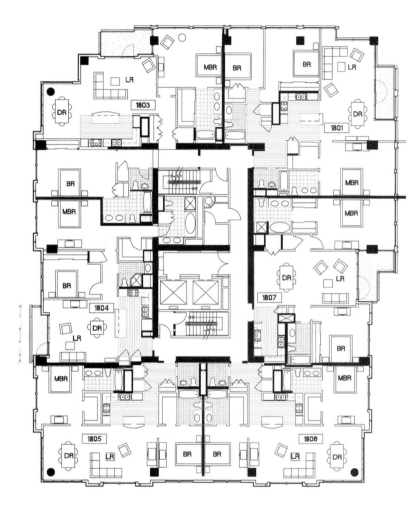

The highest levels of the towers are two-story penthouse units. Six of these units have large outdoor decks, four on the 20th floor and two on the 22nd floor.

The City of San Diego's "Marina District Design Guidelines" require that 90 percent of units in new multifamily residential developments include a balcony. The Renaissance team petitioned the city to replace the balconies in some corner units with floor-to-ceiling operable glass walls, creating "convertible rooms." These units were considered the most desirable by buyers.

Targeted for the high end of the market, Renaissance units have high ceilings and dramatic views of the San Diego Bay and the skyline.

RENAISSANCE, San Diego, California
Owner / Developer: L&L Center, LLC
Master planner: Carrier Johnson Architects
Architect: Carrier Johnson Architects
Contractor: Roel Construction Company
Key consultants:
    Structural: KPFF Consulting Engineers
    Mechanical and plumbing: McParlane & Associates
    Electrical: Berg Electric
    Consulting electrical: ILA & Zammit Engineering Group
    Landscape architect: EDAW, Inc.
Project description: Urban mixed-use, consisting of two 22-story residential towers above multilevel retail and dining
Project size: 636,500 total sq ft, including 12,635 sq ft of retail commercial space and a 156,800 sq ft parking garage
Completion date:
    Phase I: October 2002
    Phase II: June 2003
Number of units: 218

▲ A typical floor plan from Reniassance's upper floors, with two- and three-bedroom flats.

with recessed windows; the southeast elevations, facing the marina, express the city's modernity with a curtain wall of glass and steel. These glassy elevations were designed to evoke greenhouses floating above the garden.

At street level, two-story townhouses provide an urban living option, opening directly to the sidewalk. Similar two-story lofts are located above, entered from the garden plaza. Occupying floors 5–19 of the towers are one-, two-, and three-bedroom flats (900–1,878 sq ft in size).

Unit types:

Two-story walk-ups on the south and west sides

Two-story lofts at the garden level 20 ft above the street

One-, two-, and three-bedroom units on the 5th through 19th floors of towers

Two-story penthouses on the 20th and 22nd floors

Amenities: Terraced garden with outdoor pool and spa; exercise room; multipurpose meeting room

Site size: 200' × 300' (60,000 sq ft)

Density: 156 dwelling units per acre

Floor area ratio: 7.0

Parking: The garden sits atop the parking structure two stories above street level, and the structure itself is surrounded by multi-level townhomes, retail, and garden terraces.

470 parking spaces

Four stories: two above grade, two below grade

▲ *This typical two-bedroom tower unit at Renaissance has a balcony with views of the San Diego bay and skyline. Carrier Johnson Architects.*

▶ Retail occupies several floors at the base of the tower. All the residential units above have views. Gary Edward Handel + Associates. Photo by Andrew Gordon.

▶ Lincoln Triangle's site is the triangle formed by the intersection of Broadway and Columbus Avenue in New York City. Gary Edward Handel + Associates. Photo by Tom Reiss.

Lincoln Triangle
New York City

The Lincoln Triangle tower is part of Lincoln Square, a four-building complex built by a developer-architect team between 1994 and 1999 in New York City. The four buildings contain over 2.2 million sq ft and include residential, hotel, retail, theater, and

fitness club uses. Located on the Upper West Side of Manhattan, just north of Lincoln Center (for which it is named), the design of the complex is intended to smooth the transition between the residential Upper West Side and the Lincoln Center cultural district.

Lincoln Triangle is a 32-story, mixed-use residential tower completed in 1995. Its site is a triangle formed by the intersection of Broadway and Columbus Avenue.

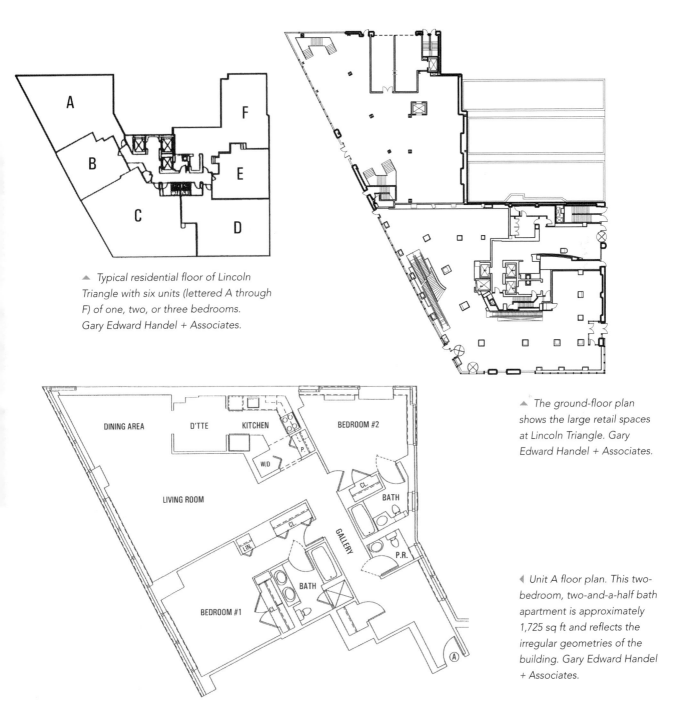

▲ Typical residential floor of Lincoln Triangle with six units (lettered A through F) of one, two, or three bedrooms. Gary Edward Handel + Associates.

▲ The ground-floor plan shows the large retail spaces at Lincoln Triangle. Gary Edward Handel + Associates.

◀ Unit A floor plan. This two-bedroom, two-and-a-half bath apartment is approximately 1,725 sq ft and reflects the irregular geometries of the building. Gary Edward Handel + Associates.

135

▲ The Lincoln Triangle building is sheathed in buff-colored brick with cast-stone sills, operable aluminum windows, and a granite base. Gary Edward Handel + Associates. Photo by Andrew Gordon.

Design

The building consists of a four-story retail base, including Barnes & Noble's 65,000 sq ft flagship store. Above the retail base there are 23 typical residential and four penthouse floors. The exterior envelope is composed of buff-colored brick, cast-stone sills, operable aluminum windows, and a granite base.

Development

Lincoln Triangle brings a suburban program type—big-box retail—into the city to occupy the base of the building and stacks a slim residential tower on top. The suburban model of inward-looking big-box stores with huge blank walls to the outside is reversed: this store opens to the outside via glass walls. The idea of an open box enclosed by glass walls extends the sidewalk inside and redefines the public realm.

High-rise residential buildings often combine just one or two floors of retail with apartments above. Only the mid-and high-level apartments, situated above the street noise and with better views, yield a higher return per square foot. By substituting large-volume retail for apartments at the lower levels, all of the apartments at Lincoln Triangle are given good views, and the mix of uses reinforces both the apartments' and the retail spaces' appeal and market value.

LINCOLN TRIANGLE, *New York City*
Owner / Developer: Millennium Partners
Master planner: Gary Edward Handel + Associates
Architect:
  Design architect: Gary Edward Handel + Associates
  Architect of record: Schuman Lichtenstein Claman Efron Architects
Contractor: Bovis Lend Lease

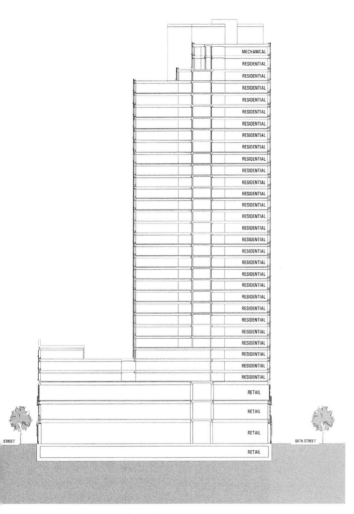

▲ Section showing the building's mixed uses.
Gary Edward Handel + Associates.

▲ *Lincoln Triangle, as seen from the corner of West 67th Street and Broadway, showing the retail space in the foreground and the tower in the background. Gary Edward Handel + Associates. Photo by Tom Reiss.*

Key consultants:
  Structural: DeSimone Consulting
  Engineers
  Mechanical: IM Robbins Consulting
  Engineers
Project description: Urban, mixed-use tower

Completion date: 1995
Number of units / type / size: 143 units;
320,000 total sq ft
Site size: 20,110 sq ft
Density: 104 units per acre
Parking: None

▶▶ *The second floor includes both residential units and the headquarters of the Battery Park City Parks Conservancy. © Pelli Clarke Pelli Architects.*

▼ *The Visionaire is a LEED Platinum residential building in Battery Park City, one of Manhattan's densest residential neighborhoods. © Pelli Clarke Pelli Architects.*

Visionaire
New York, New York

The Visionaire is a Leadership in Energy and Environmental Design (LEED) Platinum residential building in Battery Park City that combines luxury living with sustainable design.

The building has a 10-story base supporting a 35-story tower. The mixed-use program consists of 251 condominium units, street-level retail, underground parking, and the headquarters for the Battery Park City Parks Conservancy. Amenities for residents include a health club, lap pool, and children's playroom.

The Visionaire is the third of three projects produced by a collaboration between the same developer and architectural team. Lessons learned from the earlier two, including data provided by their operational managers, helped to advance the sustainability standards of the Visionaire.

Site design and parking
The site is located close to three major transportation resources: several subway and bus lines, water transportation, and a bike

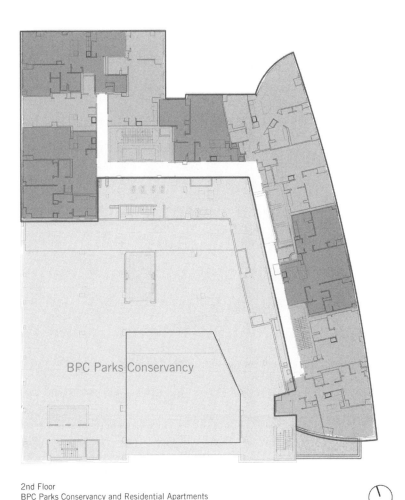

2nd Floor
BPC Parks Conservancy and Residential Apartments

0   25'   50'

path. Parking spaces are provided in an underground garage that also contains a recharge area for electric cars. Storage for 125 bicycles is provided inside the base of the building.

Building design

The most prominent feature of the Visionaire's design is its curved-glass and terra-cotta facade. The base is rectilinear and conforms to the perimeter of the city block, while the faces of the tower have more expressive shaping. The horizontal bands of windows were designed to maximize panoramic views and natural light. Spans of operable casement windows of floor-to-ceiling low-E insulated glazing provide accents on the facade. Bands of terra-cotta rain screen alternate with the curtain wall glazing. The curtain wall was prefabricated in

▲ The curving face of the tower is a prominent design feature. At the base, granite bands border low-iron glass panels to form storefront windows and building entries. © Pelli Clarke Pelli Architects.

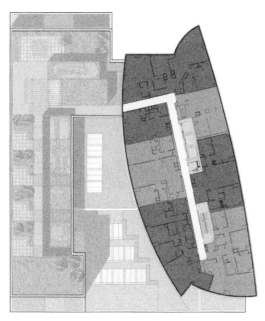

11th Floor
Residential Tower Apartments and Recreational Garden

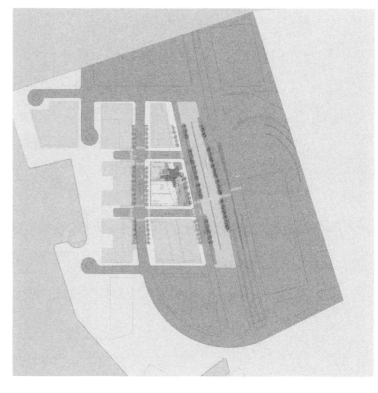

▲ The 11th-floor plan shows units in the tower and the adjacent recreational roof garden. © Pelli Clarke Pelli Architects.

◀A bike path is situated to the east of the building, and subway, bus, and water transportation are available within a short walk. © Pelli Clarke Pelli Architects.

approximately 4 ft × 11 ft sections, for performance and installation efficiency. At the base, granite bands border low-iron glass panels to form storefront windows and building entries. A portion of the tower bulkhead incorporates 4,500 sq ft of photovoltaic cells, providing 45 kW of power. It is a small percent of the building's energy need, but the panels provide highly visible expression of the project's sustainable intent.

The uppermost roof carries a shallow layer of soil that supports low-lying plants with minimal maintenance needs, while lower roof areas have deeper soil depths and a wider variety of vegetation, along with recreational garden and deck areas. Permeable and high-albedo paving materials are used to improve rain absorption and solar reflectance.

Both the roof greenery and choice of paving materials help to mitigate the heat-island effect as well as improve storm-water collection. Storm-water retention and wastewater treatment are located together below grade, where water is filtered and cleaned to maximize possible reuse and minimize impact on the city storm-water and sewage systems.

The Visionaire's overall water efficiency is significant (40%) in comparison to a typical, code-compliant building: all plumbing fixtures are low-flow, and the building's water supply incorporates the treated storm water and wastewater for use in toilets and the central air-conditioning's evaporative cooling.

The central outside-air system of the Visionaire delivers filtered, conditioned fresh air directly to bedrooms and living rooms within

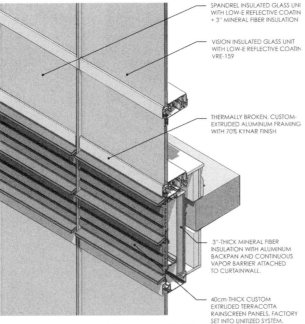

OVERALL TOTAL ASSEMBLY OF
WALL INCLUDING INTERIOR
FURRING AND INSULATION:
R-VALUE 20

SPANDREL INSULATED GLASS UNIT
WITH LOW-E REFLECTIVE COATIN
+ 3" MINERAL FIBER INSULATION

VISION INSULATED GLASS UNIT
WITH LOW-E REFLECTIVE COATIN
VRE-159

THERMALLY BROKEN, CUSTOM-
EXTRUDED ALUMINUM FRAMING
WITH 70% KYNAR FINISH

3"-THICK MINERAL FIBER
INSULATION WITH ALUMINUM
BACKPAN AND CONTINUOUS
VAPOR BARRIER ATTACHED
TO CURTAINWALL.

40cm-THICK CUSTOM
EXTRUDED TERRACOTTA
RAINSCREEN PANELS, FACTORY
SET INTO UNITIZED SYSTEM.

AXONOMETRIC SECTION OF CURTAINWALL ENVELOPE

each apartment. This system, rare among multifamily residential buildings, contributes to the Visionaire's exceptional indoor air quality (IAQ). The system delivers heated and humidified air during colder conditions or cooled and dehumidified air during hotter conditions. Operable windows also allow residents to control direct outdoor ventilation. Interior finishes give off low levels of volatile organic compounds (VOCs) and also contribute to the building's exceptional IAQ.

The Visionaire is designed to be 42 percent more energy efficient than a typical, code-compliant building. This efficiency is enhanced with a variety of on-site alternative energy systems, including: two 1,500 ft deep geothermal wells that provide heating and cooling for offices of the Battery Park City Parks Conservancy's (40,000 sq ft of space located in the building); a rooftop, natural-gas-fired microturbine that generates 60 kW electricity while simultaneously providing heat for domestic hot water for much of the building; and integrated photovoltaic panels, as previously noted. The building's general heating, ventilating, and air-conditioning (HVAC) system is powered by natural gas, which reduces peak electricity demand for the building and the city's power grid. The building management purchases 39 percent of the building's required energy from wind farms.

▲ Bands of terra-cotta rain screen alternate with the curtain wall glazing.
© Pelli Clarke Pelli Architects.

▼ An axonometric section of the curtain wall envelope, including thermally broken aluminum framing and terra-cotta rain-screen panels.
© Pelli Clarke Pelli Architects.

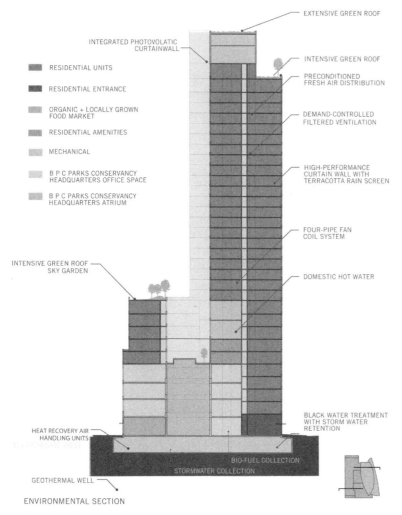

EXTENSIVE GREEN ROOF

INTEGRATED PHOTOVOLATIC CURTAINWALL

INTENSIVE GREEN ROOF

PRECONDITIONED FRESH AIR DISTRIBUTION

RESIDENTIAL UNITS

RESIDENTIAL ENTRANCE

ORGANIC + LOCALLY GROWN FOOD MARKET

RESIDENTIAL AMENITIES

MECHANICAL

B P C PARKS CONSERVANCY HEADQUARTERS OFFICE SPACE

B P C PARKS CONSERVANCY HEADQUARTERS ATRIUM

DEMAND-CONTROLLED FILTERED VENTILATION

HIGH-PERFORMANCE CURTAIN WALL WITH TERRACOTTA RAIN SCREEN

FOUR-PIPE FAN COIL SYSTEM

DOMESTIC HOT WATER

INTENSIVE GREEN ROOF SKY GARDEN

BLACK WATER TREATMENT WITH STORM WATER RETENTION

HEAT RECOVERY AIR HANDLING UNITS

BIO-FUEL COLLECTION

STORMWATER COLLECTION

GEOTHERMAL WELL

ENVIRONMENTAL SECTION

▲ The Visionaire incorporates many sustainable features, such as green roofs, geothermal wells, and wastewater treatment. © Pelli Clarke Pelli Architects.

VISIONAIRE New York, New York

Owner / Developer: The Albanese Organization

Owner Partner: Starwood Capital Group

Design Architect: Pelli Clarke Pelli Architects

Associate Architect: SLCE Architects

Contractor: Turner Construction Company

Key consultants:

Structural: DeSimone Consulting Engineers

Mechanical and plumbing: Cosentini Associates

Electrical: Cosentini Associates

Landscape architect: Coen & Partners

Sustainability: Atelier Ten

Project description: Urban mixed-use; 35-story residential condominium tower including a 10-story base with residential amenities, organic food market, public park administrative offices, and underground parking

Project size: 450,000 total sq ft

Completion date: 2008

Number of units / type:

251 units

Studio, one-, two-, and three-bedroom, penthouse

Amenities: Pool, fitness center, spa, children's playroom, roof gardens

Site size: 35,352 sq ft

Building footprint: 27,663 sq ft

Density: 374 dwelling units per acre

Parking: 100 parking spaces underground

1 Net space is the area devoted to actual living space; gross space is the total area of the building, including stairs, halls, mechanical space, et cetera. The exact definitions of these terms vary in different codes and regulatory or real estate documents. When discussing these terms, it is important to make sure that they are clearly defined.

CHAPTER 7

ADAPTIVE REUSE

Adaptive reuse for housing is the conversion of older structures built for other uses into residential space. This covers a broad spectrum of building types: warehouses, breweries, mills, schools, hospitals, and office buildings, to name a few. In a trend fueled by the growing popularity of urban living, these older structures are being redeveloped into condominiums, co-ops, and rental apartments. Most of these conversions are concentrated in areas where population shifts and economic changes have left empty buildings and where there is now a market for housing. For developers, adaptive reuse provides the opportunity to develop in locations of inherent value such as urban centers, walkable neighborhoods, or existing commercial districts where infrastructure is already in place.

Thus, despite the difficulties associated with renovation, many developers are eager to create unique projects, preserve historic structures, and possibly spearhead rejuvenation of a neglected part of the city. *Historic* buildings are those that should be preserved for their architectural or historic value. They may be protected by a listing in the National Register of Historic Places or by a local designation, covering either the exterior only or (in special cases) some interior features as well. *Old* buildings, on the other hand, may be functional and interesting, but they do not have the importance of historic buildings and can generally be modified more dramatically on the exterior as well as in the interior. Although there is greater freedom in converting old buildings to completely new uses, historic buildings can create spectacular housing with radical changes on the interior and restoration and preservation on the exterior.

BACKGROUND

The reuse of buildings for new purposes goes back for centuries: castles have become museums, convents and palaces have become hotels, and what was once a Roman theater was converted to housing (in Lucca, Italy). A well-built building may have many lives.

▼ *The Roman theater in Lucca, Italy, has housed apartments (upper floors) and restaurants and shops (ground floor) since the Middle Ages. Photo by Jean Lawrence.*

The 1960s conversion of the Prince Spaghetti Factory into luxury apartments on Boston's waterfront (by the firm Anderson Notter Finegold Associates) was at the forefront of the move to turn industrial space into high-end housing, but artists have been renovating industrial space for live-work lofts for generations. Whereas artists moved to remote locations to find inexpensive housing and large studio space, much of today's adaptive reuse housing is marketed to upper-income residents for its special features. Also, many cities want to encourage housing in or near older downtown areas for the life it brings after normal business hours.

CODE AND REGULATORY ISSUES

Strict building codes, especially fire codes, have in the past made the use of existing buildings for housing difficult. Regulations may also require additional work for renovations that is not needed for new construction. For example, if an older structure contains asbestos or other hazardous materials, these must be sealed or removed to comply with environmental regulations. Similarly, an industrial site may have contaminated soils that require remediation. Because city, state, and federal agencies now encourage conversion of old offices, hotels, and other buildings to multifamily residences to enliven downtowns, they may offer a variety of incentives for renovation. These include the relaxation of regulatory barriers (easing or making more flexible certain aspects of the codes) and tax incentives.

A number of jurisdictions have in recent years enacted initiatives intended to encourage adaptive reuse and historic preservation. Examples of these initiatives include:

- Pedestrian-oriented developments (PODs) and unified parking districts have been implemented by many municipalities. These are special zoning classifications that allow parking to be removed from new housing units but located within walking distance and shared inside a specified district, such as a downtown. This can help with a common impediment to reuse in urban areas, where parking may be required for each unit but adding new parking in or adjacent to an existing building is often infeasible. For example, Los Angeles liberalized parking requirements downtown and allowed more flexibility in the size and layout of living spaces. Seattle relaxed or waived parking requirements for certain historic structures.
- The U.S. Department of Housing and Urban Development developed rehabilitation standards called the Nationally Applicable Recommended Rehabilitation Provisions (NARRP), which could serve as a national model for "smart codes"— building and construction codes that encourage the reuse of existing buildings. For example, New Jersey developed a new state building code specifically to govern the rehabilitation of existing buildings.
- The federal government offers tax incentives for the conversion of historic buildings to rental apartments. Developers may use federal historic-preservation tax credits to cover a percentage of the project cost or may sell the credits to investors in exchange for equity. In return for historic designation, a developer agrees to limitations, particularly on changes on the exterior of the building. Some municipalities

may also be willing to provide a simple tax abatement for some period of time to help make a reuse project feasible.

GENERAL DESIGN CONSIDERATIONS

Mixed-Use Possibilities
Large commercial, institutional, or industrial complexes built in the last century frequently incorporate a number of different building volumes. This variety of building forms suggests redeveloping them to accommodate a diversity of housing types and other uses. For example, a number of historic train stations across the United States have been renovated as mixed-use developments with housing, hotels, transit stations, retail, and public parking. Another approach was taken in New Orleans, Louisiana, at the 323,000 sq ft Cotton Mill in the Warehouse District, which was converted into nearly 300 rental apartments and condominium units. The complex comprises six 3- and 4-story structures enclosing a half-acre courtyard; several smaller structures were removed from the courtyard to open it to natural light and make room for a swimming pool, pergola, and raised stage that sits on an old foundation.

Irregular Layouts and Special Opportunities
Many commercial, institutional, and industrial buildings have deeper floor plates and higher floor-to-ceiling heights than conventional apartment buildings. Fitting new dwelling units in these buildings may require what could be considered inefficient layouts with irregular spaces. On the other hand, these unusual configurations can be more spacious and interesting than units in con-

ventional residential buildings, at no additional cost. Moreover, many older structures have an abundance of hidden spaces (e.g., basements and large attics) that may be used for additional units, special amenities (like health clubs), or remote storage space for the dwelling units. Partial demolition can be useful in older buildings, particularly those that are too deep for housing units.

Multiple Apartment Types
Offering many different dwelling unit types to adapt to the eccentricities of an older building may increase marketability and appeal to a wide range of individuals with different space requirements. An example can be found in the old Queen Anne High School renovation in Seattle, Washington; the renovation includes 39 different apartment layouts. (See p. 157 for a case study of this project.)

▲ *At the Cotton Mill in New Orleans, Louisiana, selective demolition of structures has opened the courtyard for light, views, and recreation space for the residents. Developer: Historic Restoration, Inc. Architect of record and contractor: HCI Construction and Design. Architect: Gary Meadows. Photo by Rick Olivier Photography.*

▶ This grand arched window from the original 1909 Queen Anne High School building in Seattle, Washington, has been incorporated into new housing; it is a desirable feature that, in some units, allows a spectacular view of downtown Seattle and the Space Needle. Photo by Bumgardner Architecture + Interiors + Planning.

Offering numerous floor plans of different sizes tends to produce wide price ranges and gives buyers more options; but this variety can be more expensive to design and build. Some developers, especially in the case of luxury condominiums, transfer this expense to individual buyers by selling dwelling units as "shell and core." Building-wide systems are provided as part of these projects, but the individual apartments are empty spaces to be finished by the buyers.

Importance of Early Analysis and Testing Layouts

Residential adaptive reuse projects usually involve gutting interior partitions and re-placing all mechanical systems. It is there-fore critical to analyze the structural system and basic core design and to test layouts of

housing units to determine whether the building is a spatially and financially realistic candidate for conversion before committing to a project. The analysis should also determine which elements of the building must be left in place and which may be changed without excessive cost.

Integrating New Mechanical Systems

Installing modern systems (including plumbing pipes, electrical wiring, and duct-work for heating and cooling) in older structures presents special challenges beyond those associated with new housing (see discussion in Chapter 8, "Building Systems"). A major challenge in renovating a building whose interior finishes and features will be retained lies in determining how to weave these modern systems into the building's

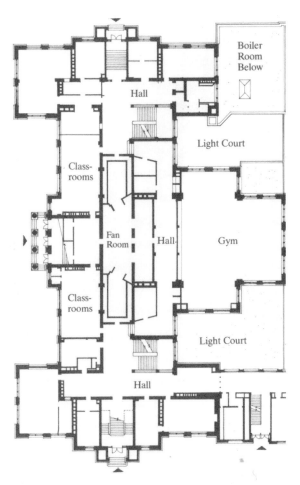

Before Conversion

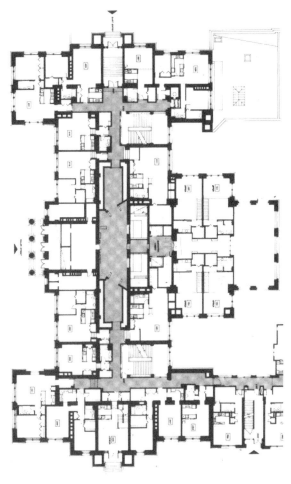

After Conversion

fabric; new systems may be very difficult to hide in older structures not designed with space to accommodate them. Creativity and very close coordination among the architect, engineers, and contractor during design and construction are required. Under the right circumstances, some of these elements can be exposed and made design features, but this also entails very careful coordination and often additional expense (to route the systems as desired and make surfaces that are not usually seen visually appealing).

CONVERSION ISSUES FOR SPECIFIC BUILDING TYPES

Industrial Buildings

Many older warehouses and other industrial buildings are suitable for redevelopment as urban loft units for artists who want to combine their living and working space or for others who like that ambiance. Deep floor plates, high ceilings (up to 20 ft), and oversized windows provide excellent daylight and allow individuals to shape the space to

▲ *A wide variety of floor plans is often required to create workable dwelling units in buildings converted from other uses. These plans show the variety of unit types (after conversion) carved out of the original (before conversion) Queen Anne High School in Seattle. Bumgardner Architecture + Interiors + Planning.*

▷ Exposing mechanical systems can create an appealing high-tech aesthetic in old industrial buildings. The Cotton Mill, New Orleans, Louisiana. Developer: Historic Restoration, Inc. Architect of record and contractor: HCI Construction and Design. Architect: Gary Meadows. Photo by Rick Olivier Photography.

their own specifications. These loft conversions often have exposed masonry walls, wood (or sometimes concrete) floors, and exposed ductwork, recalling their industrial past. The unit configurations may take advantage of the large volumes, with mezzanines (often for bedrooms) and/or freestanding kitchen and bath islands within the space. This type of apartment has become so popular in many cities that, having exhausted the supply of existing warehouses, developers are now building all-new loft-style apartments.

Office Buildings

A sweeping view of the landscape, whether urban or rural, is often one of the amenities of luxury residential living. This makes office towers good candidates for residential conversions. In addition, office buildings usually have higher ceilings (with room to run ducts) and larger structural grids than typical multifamily residential buildings. In the case of many older office towers, such features as multistory lobbies with luxurious materials and ornate detailing can be strong marketing draws.

Schools

Urban schools, frequently located in residential neighborhoods close to shopping areas and services, are good candidates for residential conversion. Many of these developments have been targeted to older residents, giving them the option of downsizing without having to leave their neighborhoods and possibly allowing them to walk to town. Since a typical 900 sq ft classroom makes a good one-bedroom apartment, schools can be quite easy to reconfigure as housing.

▲ *Tent City, Boston, MA. A shared courtyard with townhouse-style buildings on right and left, with a stepped midrise in the background. Goody Clancy. Photo: Steve Rosenthal.*

▶ *Borneo Sporenburg, Amsterdam, Netherlands. At the canal-style row houses of Borneo Sporenburg, water becomes the public domain. The waterside side of the houses also provides a docking space, creating an alternate means of transportation. West 8. Photo: Jeroen Mulsch.*

▼ *The Queen Anne, Seattle, WA. The Queen Anne is a successful conversion of a historic high school to a lively housing complex. Inspired by late-Renaissance English palaces, the Queen Anne's remarkable architecture is visible from numerous points in Seattle. Bumgardner Architecture + Interiors + Planning.*

▶ *Beddington Zero Energy Development (BedZED) New English Garden City, Sutton, United Kingdom. View of the larger townhouses at BedZED, which is a near carbon-neutral, live/work community. Its townhouses, constructed primarily of recycled materials, set a positive example for sustainable design. Bill Dunster Architects ZEDfactory Ltd. Photo: Raf Makda; © Raf Makda/VIEW.*

▲ The Exchange, New York City. The Exchange was Lower Manhattan's first office-to-residential conversion project. The building combines elegance and convenience with its historic details and modern amenities. At its ground level, a restaurant and market/ café offer residents a gourmet selection of food and a view of the New York Stock Exchange. Costas Kondylis & Associates, PC. Photo: courtesy Crescent Heights of America.

▶ Langham Court, Boston. View of the exterior, looking into the courtyard. Bay windows, multicolored brick, and stoops enliven the neighborhood's architecture. Goody Clancy. Photo: Steve Rosenthal; © Steve Rosenthal.

▲ Harbor Steps, Seattle, Washington. "Hammering Man" (Jonathan Borofsky), a popular sculpture at the nearby Seattle Art Museum, overlooks one of the four towers that comprise the Harbor Steps Apartments. Hewitt Architects. Photo: Dennis Baerwald.

▶ Lincoln Triangle, New York City. Lincoln Triangle is a mixed-residential high-rise in the heart of Manhattan's Upper West Side. Its innovative design synthesizes residential and retail uses within a thriving urban center. Gary Edward Handel + Associates. Photo: Tom Reiss.

▲ Mizner Park, Boca Raton, Florida. Two-thirds of Mizner Park is devoted to public areas including broad public walkways, park areas, and a landscaped village green, sprinkled with gazebos, benches, and fountains. The Mizner Park fountains and gazebos have become area landmarks and popular gathering places for locals and tourists alike. Cooper Carry, Inc. Photo: Gabriel Benzur Photography.

◀ Renaissance, San Diego, California.
Renaissance combines luxury high-rise living and natural elements to create an urban garden community in downtown San Diego. Carrier Johnson. Photo: Ann Garrison.

▲ Yerba Buena Lofts, San Francisco. Located in San Francisco's South of Market district, the Yerba Buena lofts offer double-height lofts for residential use with open floor plans, terraces, and bays. Stanley Saitowitz Office/Natoma Architects, Inc. Photo: Tim Griffith.

▲ Prairie Crossing, Grayslake, Illinois. The distinctive landscaping at Prairie Crossing relies on native prairie plants whose deep roots prevent erosion and flooding. Prairies are maintained by periodic controlled burns, which are far less expensive than mowing lawns. Prairie Holdings Corporation. Photo: Victoria Post Ranney.

▶ La Brea Franklin Family Housing, Los Angeles. One of four courtyards that serves as a gathering space for a community of ten households. Santos Prescott and Associates. Photo: David Hewitt/Anne Garrison.

◀ Colorado Court, Santa Monica, California. Colorado Court contains 44 units of affordable, single-room occupancy housing near transit and downtown services, and is a highly recognizable example of sustainable design. The neutral stucco walls contrast with the deep purple color of the polycrystalline solar panels. Photo: Marvin Rand.

▲ Morgan Woods, Edgartown, Massachusetts. Buildings in this affordable housing development are designed to look like large single-family homes, but they all contain multifamily units. Photo: Bruce T. Martin, ©www.bruceTmartin.com.

◀ Swan's Marketplace, Oakland, California. A central courtyard provides gathering space for this vibrant urban community. Photo: Pyatok Architects, Inc.

▼ Danielson Grove, Kirkland, Washington. Each house at Danielson Grove faces a landscaped common courtyard. The common house is at the far end. Ross Chapin Architects, www.rosschapin.com.

◀ Tango, Malmö, Sweden. Vibrantly colored towers "dance" around the courtyard at Tango. Wooden boardwalks over the marsh vegetation lead to the center island which functions as a shared social space. Photo: Werner Huthmacher, Berlin.

▶ *The Visionaire, New York City. The curving façade of this luxury high-rise juxtaposes ribbons of terra cotta with insulated, high-reflecting glass and a photovoltaic array near the top of the tower. Photo: ©Pelli Clarke Pelli Architects.*

PLANNING, SITE ISSUES, AND PARKING

Schools are attractive for residential conversion not only for their location in neighborhoods, commonly near existing services, but also for their sizable schoolyards or play areas, which can provide outdoor space and parking. Residential conversions of commercial and industrial buildings, on the other hand, may have to overcome additional site obstacles. Many commercial districts do not offer nearby groceries, pharmacies, dry cleaners, and other services. To attract residential tenants, therefore, a developer may need to offer amenities such as health facilities, restaurants, and new retail space.

Parking is dictated both by a local jurisdiction's requirements and by market expectations. Some cities require only a fraction of a space per unit and others as many as

one space per bedroom. There should be lower parking requirements in locations close to public transportation; some cities also relax or waive parking requirements for historic buildings. But even when local codes require few spaces, developers often want to provide more to meet the demands of the market. For example, empty nesters who have moved downtown from the suburbs and are accustomed to driving may want the convenience of on-site parking.

Historic buildings located in central business districts may not have space for on-grade parking or even a conventional garage. In this case, expensive alternatives may have to be considered. Parking may be accommodated in the basement or the first several floors of a building, ideally masked by retail space facing the street. If a building is large enough, parking may be buried within the

▲ *A restored office building lobby makes an impressive entry for housing in New York City. Costas Kondylis & Associates, PC. Photo by Crescent Heights of America.*

▶ Historic buildings often have a level of detail and craftsmanship that cannot be duplicated today in residential buildings. Photo by Bumgardner Architecture + Interiors + Planning.

structure with dwelling units wrapping it (see the illustration on p. 98). Adequate ventilation must be provided, and the structural system of an existing building must be analyzed, and possibly reinforced, to allow for parking. A few developers have installed underground mechanical stacking systems in historic buildings on very tight urban sites. These mechanical parking systems require a parking attendant and, although more common in Europe and Asia, have rarely been used in the United States because of their high cost.

EXTERIOR DESIGN

With adaptive reuse the exterior character of the building may be one of the attractions. Substantial work is often needed on the exterior, particularly with historic structures, but this must be done with care. The following examples suggest the kinds of exterior work an older building might require:

- Original windows will almost always need to be repaired or replaced for function and thermal efficiency. The decision about whether to repair or replicate the originals (generally required for a designated historic structure) is complex: energy use (both embedded and future use) plays a role in this decision. Changed window style or sash color has a significant impact on the appearance of the building and can be a feature in an older building with less historic value.
- Masonry typically needs cleaning, repair, or repointing. Mortar color and composition must be selected to match the existing materials and cleaning techniques tested to avoid damaging old materials.
- A new roof is usually required, particularly after new openings for vents and other mechanical requirements have been added.
- Sometimes new openings in the building structure are needed, for additional windows or balconies, while old openings may be closed.
- Rooftops may be used for shared open space or additional penthouse units, if the structure can support additional loads (as is frequently the case with former industrial buildings). For example, steel columns to support a new penthouse for the FP3 condominium in Boston's Fort Point Channel district were threaded

through the old buildings so they would not disturb the historic brick and wood interiors (see the illustration above).

SUSTAINABILITY

Adaptive reuse is an inherently sustainable practice, because the reuse of an existing building saves a good deal of energy, materials, and waste compared to demolition and new construction. Reuse also utilizes existing infrastructure so that new utility lines are not required. Ideally the buildings stand near existing transit lines, reducing the need for au-

tomobile use. An analysis of the impact of demolition (of parts of or the whole building) should consider embedded energy—that is, the energy it took to create the existing elements that would be discarded.

Before beginning the design process, it is important to evaluate a building's existing attributes. The building should be analyzed to assess the condition of the walls and roof, identify sources of air infiltration, and confirm the presence of effective vapor barriers. Existing historic features, such as porches, skylights, shutters, cupolas, and transom

▲ *The FP3 condominium complex by Hacin & Associates, located in a former industrial neighborhood of Boston, consists of two existing brick buildings, an adjacent new building designed in an updated but complementary style, and a new three-story green copper penthouse. Photo by Bruce T. Martin, © www.bruceTmartin.com.*

windows, often contribute to the energy efficiency of an historic building by shading it and inducing cross breezes in hot climates and reducing the need for artificial light in cooler climates. Care should be taken when specifying materials and installation techniques to be sure that they are compatible with existing conditions and will not harm historic materials or pose significant health and safety problems.

The site of an historic building is an important part of its context. If the building is situated in a nonurban setting, it is usually surrounded by mature existing landscaping. Special care should be taken to minimize site disturbance so as to avoid potential erosion and pollution problems, while preserving important landscape features. Adequate site drainage should be maintained to prevent damage to the building and site features.

Measures can be taken to improve the envelope's resistance to thermal energy transfer; however, they should be considered in conjunction with their effect on architectural detailing. The installation of thermal insulation between the building interior and unconditioned spaces such as attics and cellars can save energy by decreasing the loads on the mechanical systems. Single glazing can be replaced with thermal glazing in some types of existing sash windows, interior storm windows can augment historic sash

windows, or the windows may be replaced with entirely new high-performance windows if they are beyond repair. Louvers, operable windows, and historic shading devices, such as awnings, should typically be maintained to take advantage of their energy-conserving properties.

Mechanical systems should be updated and optimized for energy-efficient performance by replacing existing equipment with high-efficiency units and designing systems to the proper capacity. Original plumbing fixtures should be replaced with water-conserving fixtures such as low-flow faucets and dual-flush toilets.

Some existing materials and finishes may be hazardous and require either removal or encapsulation. Two of the most common are lead-based paint and asbestos.

It should be noted that some visible features of the original building systems may add character to the space and should be retained; for example, these may include grilles, vents, radiators, switch plates, fans, and light fixtures. Desirable views and daylighting can also be provided by existing tall windows, clerestories, and transoms. In general, older buildings were designed to be as compatible as possible with the local climate, so restoring or retaining as much of the original configuration as possible will often lend itself to optimal energy performance.

CASE STUDIES

The Exchange
New York City

The Exchange is a 21-story residential rental building named for and located near the New York Stock Exchange in lower Manhattan. Designed in 1899 by the architectural firm of Clinton & Russell, the Exchange was originally built as an office building. It was one of the first steel-frame skyscrapers in New York City and one of the most prominent buildings of its time.

In the early 1990s, the economy was in severe decline and office vacancies in the area reached as high as 30 percent. These factors, coupled with the need for an extensive overhaul, eventually left the building vacant. In 1994, the developer undertook a complete gut rehabilitation to convert the building to housing, and it reopened in 1997 as the first major office-to-residential conversion in lower Manhattan. Since its first few years of operation and despite the World Trade Center catastrophe of September 11, 2001, nearby, the Exchange has maintained an occupancy rate of close to 100 percent and has set a precedent for many other conversions in the neighborhood.

Unit design
It was originally anticipated that the building would appeal mostly to singles and young couples who worked downtown in Manhattan's financial district. However, only half of the original tenancy fell into this category. The other half of the tenants was drawn to the large, well-laid-out apartments, which are more affordable than comparable units in other luxury buildings in Manhattan.

One-bedroom units are typically 800 sq ft, while two-bedroom units average 1,200 sq ft. Floor-to-floor heights are 14 ft 0 in up to the fifth floor and 10 ft 6 in above the fifth floor, contributing to the spaciousness of the units. Units also incorporate such features as

▲ The Exchange, formerly an office building, now houses 345 luxury rental apartments in New York City. Costas Kondylis & Associates, PC. Photo by courtesy of Crescent Heights of America.

153

▶ *The living-dining area of an apartment takes advantage of the large windows and high ceilings of the former office building in lower Manhattan. Costas Kondylis & Associates, PC. Photo courtesy Crescent Heights of America.*

▼ *Typical layout for a one-bedroom unit. Costas Kondylis & Associates, PC. Courtesy Crescent Heights of America.*

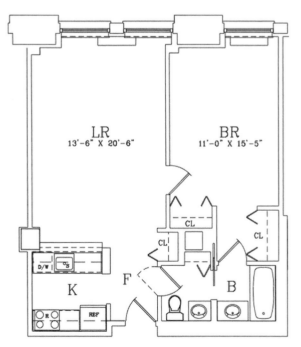

double sinks in bathrooms and "Hollywood" baths, in which a sliding door divides the room to serve as a powder room for guests.

Rehabilitation

The exterior facade of the building was preserved, the stonework scrubbed, and windows on the first four floors repaired and painted. Above the fourth floor, all windows were replaced with modern, energy-efficient units.

Inside the Exchange, finishes and details—including terrazzo floors, wood paneling, and ornate ceilings—were restored in the lobby and other public areas. Above the lobby, every floor was completely gutted, modernized, and reconfigured. The building was outfitted with electronically controlled systems, including wiring for high-speed internet access, a rarity in 1997, when the first tenants moved in. The elevator core underwent a complete rehabilitation: some shafts were eliminated to create additional floor space; the remaining five cars were refurbished with mahogany paneling.

Amenities

A large sundeck on the roof, a full-service concierge and valet, and a 24-hour doorman are provided for the tenants. In addition, since few residential services existed in this area in 1997, the developer of the Exchange included an exercise room and lap pool, conference facilities, a playroom for children, and a video rental room. A combination restaurant, market, and café was included on the first floor to serve residents and to stimulate street life in the Financial District.

THE EXCHANGE, New York City
Owner / Developer: Crescent Heights of America
Architect: Costas Kondylis & Associates, PC
Contractor: VJB Construction
Project description: High-rise conversion from office to residential

▲ The original Beaux Arts design of the lobby has been preserved. Costas Kondylis & Associates, PC. Photo courtesy Crescent Heights of America.

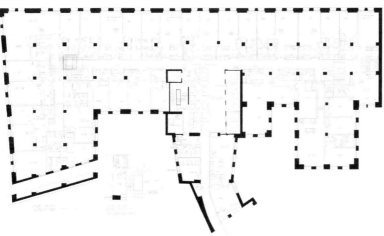

◀ Typical floor plan for floors 5 through 17. Costas Kondylis & Associates, PC. Courtesy Crescent Heights of America.

▲ A lounge below the
restaurant and market blends
contemporary design and
turn-of-the-century elements.
Costas Kondylis & Associates,
PC. Photo courtesy Crescent
Heights of America.

Completion date: January 1998
Number of units / type / size: 345 total

Unit type	sq ft	units
Studio	735–922	2
One bedroom	683–1,042	177
Two bedroom	927–1,533	145
Three bedroom	2,554–2,931	21

Site size: 0.57 acre
Density: 605 units per acre
Parking: None

The Queen Anne
Seattle, Washington

The 1909 Queen Anne High School is one of Seattle's architectural landmarks. Inspired by late-Renaissance English palaces, it is considered the finest work of architect James Stephen, designer of many Seattle schools. A 1929 addition, while somewhat simplified, remained true to the character of the original masonry facade. Two 1955 additions (for a cafeteria and an industrial arts facility), with simple, unornamented curtain walls, stand in sharp contrast to the older buildings. Taken together, the buildings illustrate a half-century's evolution in construction methods and attitudes toward educational facilities.

Queen Anne Hill overlooks downtown, approximately two miles away, and Elliott Bay. Because of its location atop the hill, the school is visible from numerous points around the city. The site is surrounded by predominantly residential buildings, including single-family houses on the south and multifamily buildings on the immediate east.

Site design

In evaluating; the existing complex, the developer-architect team determined that the 1929 auditorium and gym addition should be demolished to reveal the attractive south facade of the 1909 building. This demolition provided an open area at the center of the site, which was subsequently designed to include a grand porte cochere entrance, a pleasant formal courtyard paved with cobblestones, a circular drive with a large fountain at its center, and parking.

▼ *The Queen Anne High School was designed in 1909 by architect James Stephen. Photo by Bumgardner Architecture + Interiors + Planning.*

▶ *Over the years, additions expanded the original building. This view shows (left to right) the 1909, 1929, and 1955 buildings. Photo by Bumgardner Architecture + Interiors + Planning.*

▼ *Aerial rendering of the Queen Anne housing complex. Bumgardner Architecture + Interiors + Planning.*

The ground floor of the 1955 industrial arts addition was converted into 39 parking spaces, and the 1955 cafeteria is now 53 covered parking spaces.

Building renovation

Exterior work entailed restoring existing windows and reconfiguring the 24-in-thick masonry walls. Prior additions and breezeways were incorporated into the design.

Laying out new dwelling units in a high school, where classrooms are interspersed with laboratories and other spaces, presents a more complex redesign challenge than an elementary school, where the pattern of classrooms is often repetitive. Such a varied floor plate demanded many unit configurations to house tenants to include single parents, larger families, young professionals, and unrelated singles. Although virtually every unit has some unique feature, the 139 units come in 39 basic layouts. In contrast to standard apartments, the Queen Anne offers high-volume rooms (12 ft ceilings are typical) and

▲ The courtyard at the center of the site includes a porte cochere entrance and a fountain. Photo by Bumgardner Architecture + Interiors + Planning.

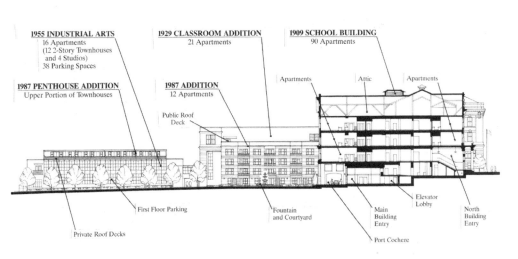

1955 INDUSTRIAL ARTS
16 Apartments
(12 2-Story Townhouses and 4 Studios)
38 Parking Spaces

1987 PENTHOUSE ADDITION
Upper Portion of Townhouses

1929 CLASSROOM ADDITION
21 Apartments

1987 ADDITION
12 Apartments

Public Roof Deck

1909 SCHOOL BUILDING
90 Apartments

Apartments   Attic   Apartments

First Floor Parking

Private Roof Decks

Fountain and Courtyard

Main Building Entry

Port Cochere

Elevator Lobby

North Building Entry

◀ This section shows the variety of apartment types in the 1909 school building. Bumgardner Architecture + Interiors + Planning.

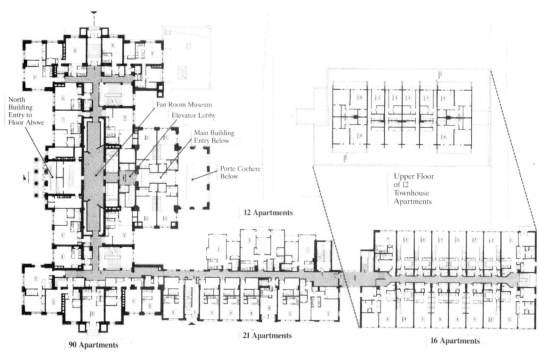

North Building Entry to Floor Above

Fan Room Museum
Elevator Lobby

Main Building Entry Below

Porte Cochere Below

12 Apartments

Upper Floor of 12 Townhouse Apartments

90 Apartments

21 Apartments

16 Apartments

N

▲ Floor plan for the second floor. High schools, with laboratories and other specialized spaces, are more complicated to convert than elementary schools. Many different unit plans are required. Bumgardner Architecture + Interiors + Planning.

▶ Architectural features of the high school, such as maple floors and chalkboards, have been preserved in the living units. Photo by Bumgardner Architecture + Interiors + Planning.

◀ This apartment has a spectacular southerly view of the Seattle skyline. Photo by Bumgardner Architecture + Interiors + Planning.

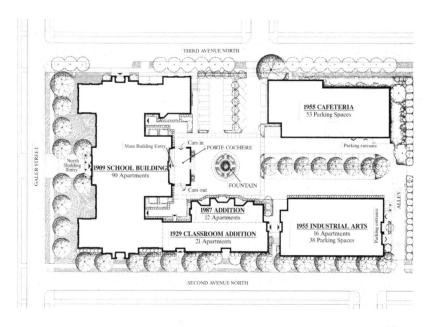

THIRD AVENUE NORTH

1955 CAFETERIA
53 Parking Spaces

Main Building Entry   Cars in   PORTE COCHERE   Parking entrance

North
Building
Entry   1909 SCHOOL BUILDING
90 Apartments   Cars out   FOUNTAIN

GALER STREET

ALLEY

1987 ADDITION
12 Apartments

1929 CLASSROOM ADDITION
21 Apartments

1955 INDUSTRIAL ARTS
16 Apartments
38 Parking Spaces

Parking entrance

SECOND AVENUE NORTH

N

▲ A site plan of the complex notes the old and new uses of each building: the 1909 school building, 1929 classroom addition, 1955 cafeteria and industrial arts buildings, and the 1987 addition. Bumgardner Architecture + Interiors + Planning.

original maple floors in many of the units. Distinctive details, such as the old chalkboards, were retained as a whimsical reminder of the building's past.

The original building was converted into 90 apartments, including loft units in a former library with a particularly high ceiling. A small, four-story addition was built onto the 1929 classroom building to accommodate 21 additional apartments.

The 1955 industrial arts addition was converted into 16 apartments—eight of which are two-level, two-bedroom units with rooftop terraces, made possible by adding a third floor. Smaller additions and breezeways were also incorporated in the design. Work on the building exteriors included restoring existing windows as well as cleaning and some reconfiguration of the thick masonry walls.

Development

In 1981, when the school was closed due to declining enrollment, the neighborhood collaborated to protect the building. Neighbors became involved early in the planning process, and a feasible alternative—converting the school into a housing complex—received strong community support. In 1984, the school district, in cooperation with the Historic Seattle Preservation and Development Authority, held a competition for plans to convert the vacant buildings for residential use. As a first step, the developer-design team succeeded in placing the school on the National Register of Historic Places, making it eligible for renovation tax credits totaling $1.6 million.

THE QUEEN ANNE, Seattle, Washington
Owner / Developer: Lorig Associates
Architect: Bumgardner Architecture + Interiors + Planning
Contractor: J. M. Rafn Company
Key consultants:
    Structural engineer: Ratti, Perbix and Clark
    Landscape architect: Robert Shinbo and Associates
Project description: Adaptive reuse and rehabilitation of an historic 1909 high school, with later additions, to house 139 moderately priced apartments
Completion date: March 1987
Number of units: 139 units, from 550 sq ft studios to 1,250 sq ft two-bedroom apartments; 39 different plan configurations
Site size: 2.85 acres
Density: 49 units per acre
Parking: 173 parking spots, 82 surface and 91 covered

Swan's Marketplace
Oakland, California

Swan's Marketplace is an adaptive reuse of an existing retail and market space into a mixed-use urban development with both condominium and rental units. The existing buildings, which occupy one whole block in the Old Oakland neighborhood, were built in stages between 1917 and 1940. An area landmark, Swan's Market was a department store and prepared-food mart for over sixty years. The renovated structure is now home to a food market, restaurants, retail, the Museum of Children's Art, office space, and 18 affordable rental units and 20 cohousing condominium units. The 3,500 sq ft common house provides additional gathering space for cohousing residents. There is a weekly farmers' market in front of the site and, at the same time, a Cultural Arts Fair takes place in the courtyard. There is also a garden in the center of the block.

▼ *The Ninth Street facade, with on-street parking and ground-floor retail flanking the entrance to Swan's Court. Pyatok Architects, Inc.*

▶ *Before and after sections reveal how the original market building was altered to create two floors plus loft space, while preserving most of the original trusswork. Pyatok Architects, Inc.*

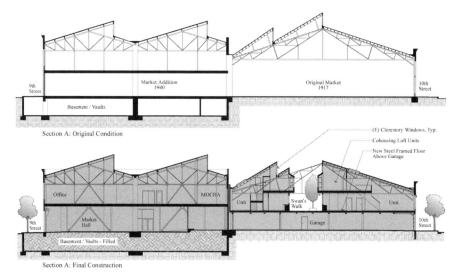

▶ *Swan's Marketplace occupies an entire city block in the Old Oakland neighborhood, once the bustling commercial center of downtown Oakland. The neighborhood declined in the early twentieth century, but in the 1980s developers recognized the demand for downtown living and entertainment and began to rehabilitate the district. Today, residents at Swan's Marketplace are within walking distance of many restaurants, stores, and other residential buildings. Pyatok Architects, Inc.*

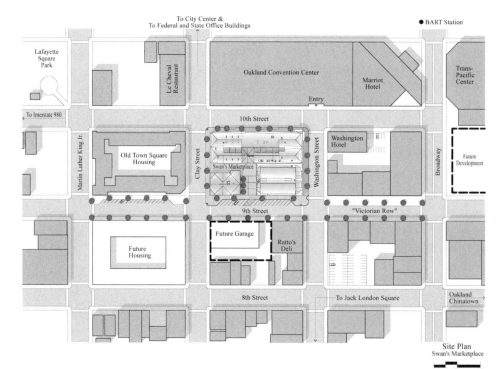

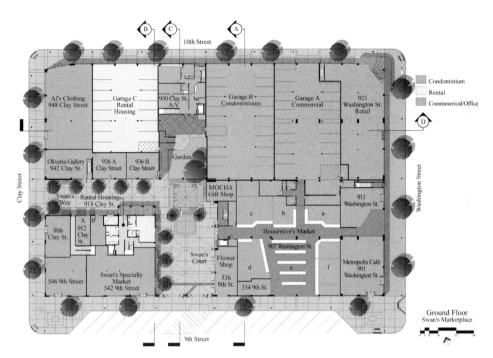

The ground floor of Swan's Marketplace incorporates parking and retail, as well as space for the historic Housewives' Market and a courtyard. Pyatok Architects, Inc.

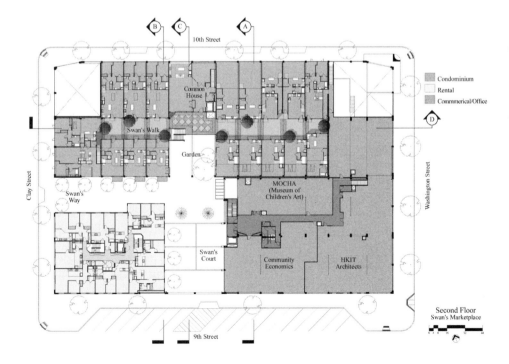

Cohousing and rental units are located on the second floor, along with the Museum of Children's Art and office space. Pyatok Architects, Inc.

▶ *Typical plans and section for a cohousing unit. Pyatok Architects, Inc.*

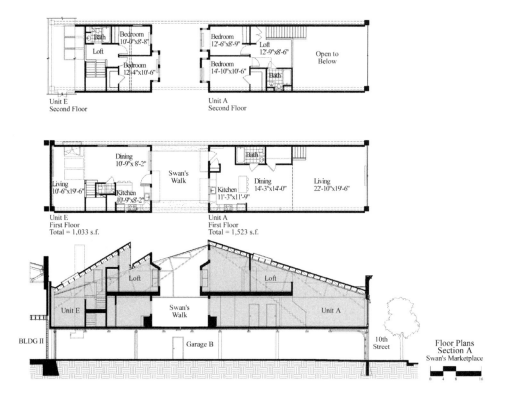

Floor Plans
Section A
Swan's Marketplace

The residential units at Swan's Marketplace are located on the second floor. The rental units are affordable to those making under 60 percent of the area median income, and the market-rate condominium units operate in the form of cohousing. Cohousing is a cooperative living arrangement under which residents own their private living spaces but share common facilities such as a group kitchen and dining area for shared meals and common outdoor space. Decisions are made by consensus of the community (often including the planning and design of the community itself). At Swan's Marketplace, shared amenities include a large kitchen and dining room, children's play room, laundry room, exercise room, workshop, guest room with bath, and extra storage space. Cohousing residents eat dinner together three nights a week and maintain an organic garden.

Site

The location initially acted as a deterrent to potential residents, because the area was marred by freeway construction and urban renewal in the 1960s and 1970s and because the neighborhood was widely seen as dangerous. Although the site also lacked any potential for green open space to be owned by the cohousing community, it did, however, provide the opportunity to live within walking distance of work places, restaurants, museums, theaters, shopping, and Chinatown.

Nearby public transportation is widely available, and the neighborhood's historic character also held appeal. The freeway construction and urban renewal that had once isolated the neighborhood had also, in a way, preserved it as a distinct remnant of the historic downtown.

The site was turned over to a nonprofit developer dedicated to affordable housing and community economic growth. The original cohousing group worked hard to attract additional members to buy into the Swan's Marketplace community. As longtime Oakland or East Bay residents, they knew that the "dangers" of the downtown area were exaggerated. They also knew they were not just buying a condo unit in an otherwise anonymous building but joining a community of people who wanted to share the experience of living downtown. Furthermore, the developer had a strong record of successful downtown projects, so potential buyers knew that their community would have long-term support.

▲ *The common house provides gathering space for the cohousing residents. Pyatok Architects, Inc.*

▶ *For over 60 years, Swan's Market was an important downtown landmark. This historic photo shows the Market in its prime.*

▼ *The building, as it looks today, at night. Pyatok Architects, Inc.*

◀ A view of Swan's Court.
Pyatok Architects, Inc.

▼ Swan's Walk is an outdoor
corridor on the second floor
between units of cohousing.
Original roof trusses span the
gap to define the space and
retain historic character.
Pyatok Architects, Inc.

Building design

The design retains 75 percent of the existing
structure, including the entire glazed brick
and terra-cotta facade. The new construction is stick-built within the historic shell.
Long-span steel trusses supported the original roof, and now portions are exposed between the two rows of condos along a
walkway known as Swan's Walk. New steel-
framed floors were added to the original
market building to create garage space on
the lower level and two-level loft units
above. Some of the existing clerestory windows were kept, and skylights were added to
the roofs to provide more light to the cohousing loft units.

A key aspect of the design is the incorporation of vibrant public spaces into the site.
The removal of portions of the roof allows
sunlight to enter the interior of the block,
and the open paved areas on the ground lev-

el provide space for markets and fairs. On the second floor, Swan's Walk provides space for cohousing residents to have seating areas in front of their units.

SWAN'S MARKETPLACE, Oakland, California

Owner / Developer: East Bay Asian Local Development Corporation

Architect: Pyatok Architects, Inc. with Y.H. Lee Associates

Contractor: Oliver & Company

Key consultants:
Structural engineers: KPA Consulting
Landscape: PGA Design
Civil engineer: Van Maren and Associates
Historian: Alan Dreyfuss
Cohousing consultant: The Cohousing Consultant

Project description: Adaptive reuse of market buildings for mixed-use development

Completion date: 2000

Project size: 30,150 sq ft

Number of units / type: 18 affordable rental units and 20 cohousing loft units

Site size: 1.38 acres

Density: 28 units per acre

Parking: 0.7 spaces per rental, 1 space per cohousing unit

CHAPTER 8
BUILDING SYSTEMS

Building systems in housing are dictated by project-specific issues such as overall size, location, site-zoning requirements, type of occupancy, and whether the housing is intended for ownership or rental. Although for the sake of clarity, this chapter separately addresses each system (e.g., structural, mechanical, electrical, plumbing and fireproofing systems, elevators, and enclosure systems), a residential unit is the assembly of numerous interrelated and interdependent elements—including foundations, exterior walls, roofing, windows and glazing, moisture protection, thermal insulation, interior partitions, interior finishes, and many more—to form a functioning, complete whole. This chapter highlights examples of the key residential building systems.

When designing building systems, it is important to consider their interaction as a whole system and to optimize the design through an integrated team approach. If design disciplines do not communicate during the design process, they will base their assumptions on the worst case and size their systems accordingly. As a result, systems will be oversized, inefficient, and will not work well together. An integrated team approach will optimize energy performance by considering mechanical systems, passive systems, natural ventilation, building envelope, lighting, fenestration, and operational control to be parts of a whole system. Following building completion, undertaking a commissioning process ensures that all systems operate as they were designed. Instructing the building operations and maintenance staff about

operations and maintenance procedures is also important to ensuring optimal performance.

REGULATORY REQUIREMENTS

All building construction is regulated by two separate sets of regulatory standards: zoning bylaws and building codes. Zoning bylaws are municipal, site-specific regulations that dictate allowable uses, densities, height, parking requirements, setbacks, and other physical requirements for the overall development of each site. While they influence the overall size and character of what can be built, they have little effect upon the requirements for the actual building systems themselves—this is the domain of building codes.

Building codes dictate the standards of construction required to maintain health, safety, and welfare and prevent or contain fire; they establish minimum performance for all materials and systems and their installation. In the United States, the International Building Code (IBC), published by the International Code Council, Inc., is rapidly being adopted by most states as the state building code. The IBC was developed in close cooperation with, and is based upon, the model codes drawn up by the Building Officials and Code Administrators International (BOCA), National Building Code, International Conference of Building Officials (ICBO), Uniform Building Code (UBC), and Southern Building Code Congress International (SBCCI) Building Code. As it is adopted by all states, the International Building Code will replace other codes and simplify code compliance from state to state. Most states also adopt or include by reference versions of the NFPA (National Fire Protection Association) codes and standards, as well as separate codes for elevator, mechanical, electrical, and plumbing work.

Building codes prescribe fire ratings for building components based on occupancy, construction type, and building area and height. For example, walls separating dwelling units from corridors, common areas, and other units (called demising walls) must be constructed to comply with code-specified minimum fire ratings. These requirements can be met with properly designed and constructed stud-demising walls that incorporate multiple layers of fire-rated gypsum wallboard. Concrete block walls also provide both fire separation and acoustical separation. Similarly, horizontal separation through use of rated floor assemblies may be required in multistory housing. Enclosures of fire stairs, elevator shafts, and piping or duct shafts also must meet minimum requirements for fire separation that vary by construction type and building size.

Although building codes contain highly restrictive requirements for all residential construction, they are less restrictive for residential buildings of three or fewer stories. Fire-suppression systems are generally required in residential buildings with more than three stories: all buildings with habitable floor levels 75 ft or more above grade are considered high-rise construction and must meet the even more stringent high-rise building code requirements. Regardless of a building's height, the choice of each building system must be made in conjunction with all other building systems, code requirements, local conditions, economics, and specific user needs.

LEADERSHIP IN ENERGY AND ENVIRONMENTAL DESIGN CERTIFICATION AND SUSTAINABILITY

As "green" building design has become a mainstream concern in residential and other building types, a new measurement of sustainability has come into widespread use. The Leadership in Energy and Environmental Design (LEED) Green Building Rating system is designed to accelerate the development and implementation of green building practices. Under this voluntary third-party system, credits are earned for satisfying specified green building criteria. LEED was developed by the U.S. Green Building Council (USGBC), a nonprofit coalition, to promote environmentally responsible and healthy places to live and work

Project evaluation covers six environmental categories: Sustainable Sites, Water Efficiency, Energy and Atmosphere, Materials and Resources, Indoor Environmental Quality, and Innovation and Design. Different levels of green building certification (Certified, Silver, Gold, and Platinum) are awarded to the finished building based on the total credits earned. Most federal agencies and many cities and states now require this certification, and the rating system is becoming recognized as a sign of environmentally responsible design.

Other green building rating systems can be used to assess a building's sustainability; the Green Building Initiative's Green Globes program is one example.

STRUCTURAL SYSTEMS

Housing construction encompasses a broad range of building sizes, shapes, and styles, ranging from the detached single-family house to the high-rise apartment tower. But whatever the form, one or a combination of the following structural systems will typically be used:

- Wood or light metal framing
- Masonry bearing wall (with concrete plank, steel deck, or wood-framed floors and roof)
- Structural steel framing (typically with composite metal deck)
- Reinforced concrete framing (with poured-in-place concrete floors)

In some instances materials are combined, and all four systems may even be used within one building. Examples of this hybrid approach include a reinforced concrete frame supporting a steel-framed roofing system, or steel beams substituted for some wood beams or trusses in a wood-framed structure to achieve long spans while reducing the overall size of the members.

Structural systems need to support the live load of the building (occupants, their furniture, and other belongings) and dead loads (the weight of the floor and wall construction itself). Building codes set standards for both live and dead loads that vary with the construction type and intended occupancy of a building. The structure and its building components also need to resist rain and/or snow load, wind loads (lateral loads and uplift), and an earthquake's seismic forces (lateral and vertical). The standards for lateral loading vary geographically, with higher wind-load requirements in areas affected by hurricanes or other storms and higher seismic loads in areas where earthquakes occur. Components in high-wind and hurricane-prone locations must also resist failure due to debris impact. This can lead to higher construction costs and impose some material limitations.

Wood and Light Metal Framing

Wood framing

Historically, housing in the United States was limited in its height and complexity. Its structure was generally a wood framing system for floors and roofs, with either either wood-stud or masonry walls. Wood is abundant, relatively inexpensive, and easily worked. Wood framing remains a commonly used system for single-family houses and low-rise housing in which spans are modest and loads fall within the capabilities of the material.

Low-rise wood construction is well within the skills of a carpenter with a helper or crew on-site and can be erected without expensive heavy equipment. Individual framing elements can be lifted and secured in place by one or two workers. In addition to structural framing, wood is often the primary material for exterior wall and roof enclosure systems, including sheathing, siding, doors, and windows. Wood is used in interior construction for interior framing and finishing. Manufactured or composite-wood products—fabricated from wood chips and/or fibers combined with synthetic resins, compressed and properly cured—produce stable, high-strength building components and sheet products. These products are now in common use in residential construction. They allow for very efficient use of material with minimal waste, but the adhesive may contain formaldehyde, a volatile organic compound (VOC) with adverse effects on indoor air quality and human health. Products that are low in formaldehyde should be specified.

Building codes limit the maximum allowable height and number of stories for wood-frame construction and specify the

▶ *Wood-frame construction requires relatively little equipment, and most components can be carried by hand and assembled by two workers. Photo by Goody Clancy.*

minimum requirements necessary to achieve the required fire classification for exterior wall construction and for the interior separation between living units, entranceways, corridors, and paths of egress. These requirements are defined in an hours-of-fire rating to protect a structural component or to limit the spread of fire from one space to another. For example, a two-hour fire rating indicates a partition that will maintain its fire integrity for two hours, before it begins to fail. Required fire ratings for interior wall systems and separations are generally achieved through the use of multiple layers of fire-rated gypsum board or, in special cases, by adding a fire-suppression system. Special detailing is required to maintain fire integrity at joints of exterior walls, roof, and foundation. Assemblies that have been tested by the Underwriters Laboratory (UL) are assigned a UL rating. The literature provided by gypsum board manufacturers illustrates rated assemblies, making reference to the UL rating.

Lateral bracing can be provided by the diaphragm action of walls themselves. The sheathing on exterior and selected interior walls, or diagonal bracing let into the walls, is often strong enough to prevent walls from being forced out of their rectilinear shape by wind or seismic forces.

While wood has long been considered the most economical and easily worked construction material for low-rise structures, it has several disadvantages. It is the most combustible of all basic structural materials.

It does not have the structural capabilities of concrete or structural steel, and in some markets a scarcity of wood makes it as costly as its chief competitors—light metal framing or concrete-block bearing walls with concrete plank floors.

Light metal framing

Light metal framing that utilizes lightweight steel studs, joists, and rafters can be an economical alternative to wood framing for single-family houses and for low-rise multiple-unit construction. Light metal members are available in a broad range of sizes and gauges; they can be ordered to size (minimizing waste), assembled like wood framing (readily sawed, screwed, welded, and reinforced), and easily handled by one or two workers. The design and assembly of light metal-framed buildings is similar to that of wood-framed structures.

Many light metal framing sections are manufactured with perforated webs to allow for mechanical and electrical distribution within the wall, roof, and floor sections being assembled. Light metal-framed panels can also be readily preassembled for easy hoisting and anchoring, either as the structural system

▲ *Light metal framing has replaced wood in many applications; assembly procedures are similar to those for wood. Photo by Goody Clancy.*

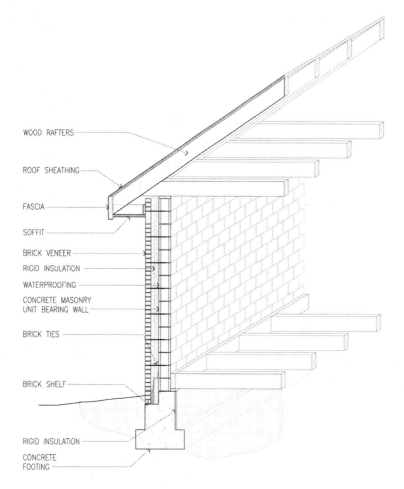

WOOD RAFTERS

ROOF SHEATHING

FASCIA

SOFFIT

BRICK VENEER

RIGID INSULATION

WATERPROOFING

CONCRETE MASONRY
UNIT BEARING WALL

BRICK TIES

BRICK SHELF

RIGID INSULATION

CONCRETE
FOOTING

▲ *Exterior masonry bearing walls supporting wood-framed floor and roof levels are an alternative to wood-frame construction. Goody Clancy.*

or as an infill panel in combination with a structural steel frame.

This framing system has become very competitive and versatile for exterior walls in buildings of all sizes when used in conjunction with structural steel frames. The light metal frame infill wall can be used instead of concrete block or masonry infill walls, greatly reducing overall weight on the structure while supporting a variety of exterior finish systems, from thin stone or brick veneers to metal

panel systems. Light metal studs are also commonly used for interior construction.

Masonry Bearing Walls and Piers

Much traditional housing has been constructed with exterior masonry bearing walls supporting wood-framed floor and roof levels, a variation of wood-framed construction. Wood posts, wood-stud walls, masonry bearing walls, or masonry piers provide interior support. Exterior masonry bearing walls remain popular; concrete block is the most common material, replacing traditional brick or stone. The floors and roofs are generally wood framing, steel framing with composite metal deck, or concrete plank (see the discussion of concrete block and plank construction below).

Today's masonry bearing walls are more sophisticated than solid walls of the past. They can include structural and seismic reinforcement, a cavity within the wall to create a thermal break, a moisture barrier, and thermal insulation. Cross-cavity ties allow for transfer of wind loads from the exterior face wall to the backup structural wall while also allowing for differential vertical movement. Masonry materials include stone, brick, other fired-clay products, and precast concrete block. These materials provide durable, economical, load-bearing vertical support. Reinforced masonry exterior walls (or interior walls between units) act as shear walls to resist lateral forces.

Steel Framing

Steel as a structural framing material emerged during the mid-nineteenth century to satisfy an increasing demand for taller buildings. As a structural framing material, steel has many important advantages:

◀ A steel-frame building under construction. Photo by Goody Clancy.

- It has the highest strength-to-weight ratio of all common building materials.
- It can be formed into a variety of structural shapes, weights, and sizes.
- It is very durable when properly protected.
- It is noncombustible, but it requires the application of fireproofing to maintain its strength in the event of fire.
- It can be recycled.

The typical steel-framed building is a post-and-beam structure with steel-framed floor and roof levels supported by steel columns that transfer all building loads to the foundation. Each floor-level frame consists of a grid of primary and secondary steel beams sized to meet the specific span and load conditions. Bar joists or other open-webbed assemblies are often substituted for steel beams to achieve longer spans with minimum weight. The open-web section provides space for the routing of pipes, ducts, and conduit, and a finished ceiling can be attached to the bottom chord of the bar joists. The actual floor plane is constructed as a composite deck, consisting typically of a 2- to 3-in. deep, 18-gauge corrugated or ribbed metal deck acting integrally with a 1.5- to 2.5-in. thick concrete topping slab. With this form of construction, a finished ceiling is usually suspended below the deck to conceal mechanical systems.

The advantage of the composite steel deck with concrete fill is that it does not require shoring during construction, since the deck acts as a form on which the concrete is

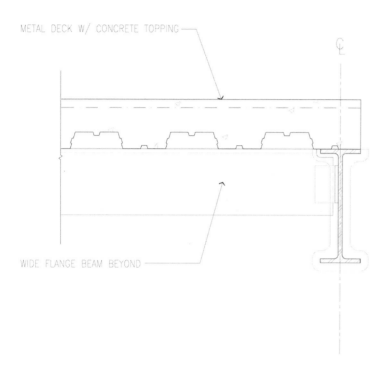

METAL DECK W/ CONCRETE TOPPING

WIDE FLANGE BEAM BEYOND

▲ *Diagram of composite deck with corrugated metal and concrete topping. Goody Clancy.*

poured. The strength of the concrete topping contributes to the structural integrity of the system when steel studs anchored to the top flange of the beams are cast into the concrete topping slab. This ensures true composite action of the structural steel frame and the concrete deck.

Steel framing, like all other framing systems, requires lateral bracing and support. This is often achieved with the use of diagonal members as integral bracing within the frame. Interior cores that accommodate elevator shafts, egress stairs, and service areas are regularly designed in such a manner as to provide additional lateral bracing and stability. A less economical alternative is a moment-frame system, where the joints between columns and beams are strength-

ened to resist lateral forces. A moment-frame system allows greater flexibility in planning, since it requires no diagonal braces.

Reinforced Concrete Framing

The third common structural system for building construction is the reinforced-concrete frame. Concrete is made by mixing cement with sand, stone aggregate, and water. The resulting hydraulic reaction creates a new stonelike material—concrete. Various cementitious materials have been known and used since the Roman Empire. In the United States, Portland cement is the primary form of hydraulic cement used as the binding agent in concrete. Fly ash or slag can be used to replace a small percent of cement in order to recycle these by-products of industrial processes.

When first mixed, concrete is a plastic material that can be formed or cast into a variety of shapes and configurations. Within a short period of time, concrete reaches an *initial set* (fixed shape or form) and then continues to cure and increase in strength in this form until it approaches its ultimate strength, typically measured after a period of 28 days. Concrete is exceptionally strong in compression, while it has less strength in tension. Since steel has high tensile capabilities, steel-reinforced concrete has been developed to maximize the advantages of both materials in combination.

Concrete-frame construction is used in mid-rise to high-rise housing but rarely in low-rise housing, except in parts of the world where wood is less available or there is high seismic risk. Concrete is more economical if the building form is repetitive and formwork can be used repeatedly; proprietary formwork systems are available that can increase the efficiency of the construction process. The frame itself resists lateral forces, and the frame and floor slabs are inherently fire resistant, requiring no additional fireproofing. Concrete also offers better sound-blocking separation between floors of a building, which is important where different families may live above each other.

A typical concrete-frame construction system generally consists of concrete columns, beams, and concrete slabs. Flat-plate construction is a variation of the concrete frame that eliminates beams and uses a thicker reinforced slab to resist. "Drops," or thickened parts of the slab around the tops of columns where shear forces are greatest, can be used to prevent what is called "column punch-through" of the slab. Because flat-plate concrete structural systems are thinner than steel-framed floors, the floor-to-floor height in concrete buildings is typically less, so that more floors can be built within an overall building height limit—often an advantage in high-rise construction where overall height is limited by code.

A demand for energy-efficient, cast-in-place concrete construction has led to a rise in the use of insulating concrete forms (ICFs), which are interlocking modular units dry stacked to form structural walls. They consist of two insulating panels (usually made of extruded polystyrene) that are connected with plastic ties and a cavity that is filled with concrete and reinforced by steel bars. The insulating panels are a permanent formwork, and the plastic ties remain permanently embedded as well. ICFs offer high insulative value as well as good fire protection and sound absorption, although their initial cost may be higher than traditional

construction methods, and they offer less flexibility for future renovation. ICFs can be used for basement foundation walls and above-grade walls in single-family and low-rise construction.

Concrete block and plank

In low-rise to mid-rise construction, pre-manufactured concrete planks are commonly used for floor construction spanning between concrete block load-bearing walls. The use of concrete plank can speed up erection time and can be economical for buildings with regular, repetitive layouts. Planks can also be used in combination with steel construction for high-rise applications. They can provide a longer span than composite deck, and fewer beams are required.

The planks are produced under quality-controlled conditions in a factory and may be less affected by weather conditions than on-site construction. However, planks are generally manufactured with an intentional camber, or slight arch, for increased strength. If the spans vary in length, the planks may not align along joints due to differences in the camber. Good practice suggests using a topping surface to conceal joints and height variations.

Concrete plank has many of the same acoustic and fire-protection advantages of poured-in-place concrete. The plank also generally serves as a finished ceiling, saving the cost of a suspended ceiling, although joints between planks are generally exposed.

With exposed plank it is necessary to find other ways to conceal systems that are generally hidden within a ceiling. Ductwork for heating and air conditioning can be run in soffits (enclosures running across ceilings generally covered with gypsum wallboard)

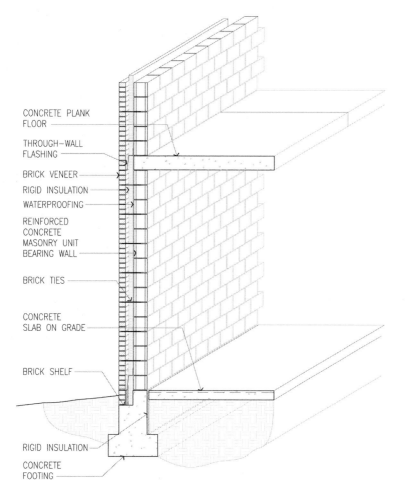

CONCRETE PLANK FLOOR

THROUGH—WALL FLASHING

BRICK VENEER

RIGID INSULATION

WATERPROOFING

REINFORCED CONCRETE MASONRY UNIT BEARING WALL

BRICK TIES

CONCRETE SLAB ON GRADE

BRICK SHELF

RIGID INSULATION

CONCRETE FOOTING

▲ *Diagram of concrete-block and premanufactured-plank construction, often used in low-rise housing construction. Goody Clancy.*

or in spaces that can tolerate lower ceiling heights. Piping and wiring can be run in the voids of bearing walls to avoid exposed pipes and wiring within the building. If ceiling-mounted light fixtures are desired, a furred gypsum board ceiling (held off the concrete plank by studs or wood strapping to provide the required space for wiring) is necessary to hide the wiring. For this reason, wall-mounted light fixtures are often used with this construction type to save the cost of adding gypsum board ceilings.

Foundations

Historically, foundations were made of stone or masonry. Since the early twentieth century, foundations are almost exclusively poured concrete, or in some cases fully grouted concrete masonry units (CMU).

Relative Costs of Structural Systems

Cost is an important factor in the selection of a structural system. Overall cost is determined not only by the expense of the material but also by regional issues, including labor and union considerations, weather conditions, and other local building conditions. Concrete is the most commonly used and economical material in some areas, steel in others. In addition, the price of structural steel fluctuates—sometimes quickly and dramatically—which changes its cost relative to concrete.

Soil conditions will determine the appropriate foundation systems, but the dead loads of concrete frame buildings are typically 40–50 percent greater than steel-framed buildings. Particularly in high-rise buildings, the difference in weight between steel and concrete construction will affect foundation costs.

Prefabricated Components

Preassembled building components produced in a factory take advantage of production-line efficiencies and reduce on-site labor and construction duration. Preassembled trusses, trussed joists, rafters, and wall panels are common. Preassembled panels often incorporate exterior finishes, sheathing, vapor barriers, thermal insulation, and sometimes preinstalled windows and doors.

Structurally insulated panels (SIPs) are an alternative to wood light-frame construction and are also used as wall and roof panels in

◀ A prefabricated wood wall being hoisted into place. Factory assembly of components may reduce costs and shorten the on-site construction schedule. Photo by Goody Clancy.

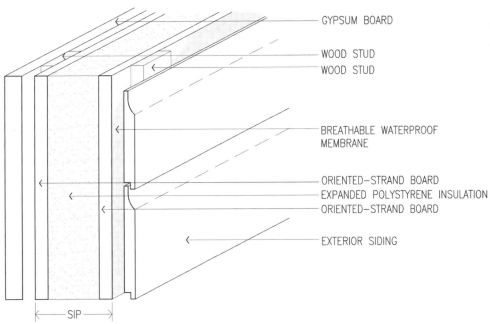

GYPSUM BOARD

WOOD STUD
WOOD STUD

BREATHABLE WATERPROOF MEMBRANE

ORIENTED-STRAND BOARD
EXPANDED POLYSTYRENE INSULATION
ORIENTED-STRAND BOARD

EXTERIOR SIDING

SIP

◀ Diagram of typical structurally insulated panel (SIP) installation. Goody Clancy.

low-rise steel-framed buildings. SIP panels consist of a layer of rigid plastic foam insulation sandwiched between two facing boards that are typically half-inch-thick oriented-strand boards (OSB). Because SIPs are insulated, they are usually used only in the building envelope or sometimes as a floor over a basement or crawl space and not in interior partitions. The panels are fabricated and precut by the manufacturer according to shop drawings and then shipped to the site when they are ready to be assembled, which can increase the speed and efficiency of the job. They are also relatively air-tight, reduce on-site waste, have almost no thermal bridges, and provide a continuous nailing surface.

A variation on SIPs is an assembly made by injecting expanding insulating foam between two pieces of sheet metal. This produces an insulated metal panel (IMP). An IMP assembly offers some benefits a typical SIP doesn't have, including metal's high durability as an exterior cladding material and its ability to accept high-performance coatings.

Prefabricated Buildings

Prefabrication building techniques have existed for centuries. More modern precedents include the Sears catalog kit homes sold from 1908 to 1940 and the steel Lustron houses of the 1940s. The most broadly successful example of contemporary prefabricated housing is manufactured housing, also known as the mobile home or trailer. These homes have a steel undercarriage to which axles and wheels can be attached for road transportation. They can be joined together on-site to create double-wide or triple-wide units.

Modular construction is a type of prefabrication that is becoming more prevalent in single-family home building and also for low- to mid-rise multifamily attached housing. A modular home is assembled in several large pieces inside a factory and then transported to the job site, where the pieces are put into place using cranes. The manufacturer installs everything from windows, walls, doors, and trim to piping, wiring, and insulation in the factory. The factory can also preinstall cabinets, appliances, light fixtures, carpets, etc. Vinyl siding can be applied in the factory, but cedar shingles or wooden clapboards are typically applied on-site. Elements that project from the building, such as decks or turrets, are also usually built on-site. The benefits of modular construction include a climate-controlled work site, faster production, and increased worker safety, but design variation is limited and there may be problems in transit, such as cracking of drywall. Chapter 3 includes a modular housing case study (p. 55).

Envelope Systems

Building envelope systems typically include insulation, an air and moisture barrier, stud framing and/or masonry units, flashing, and an exterior cladding. Traditional cladding materials include masonry veneers (stone, brick, and synthetic masonry products), wood cladding (siding, shingles, and clapboard), stucco, aluminum siding, and vinyl siding. More recently, a variety of new cladding materials has been developed, including aluminum, porcelain, and cement-board panels, and curtain wall systems. Traditionally, envelope components are separate and assembled on-site, but contemporary innovations in envelope systems combine several elements in prefabricated systems.

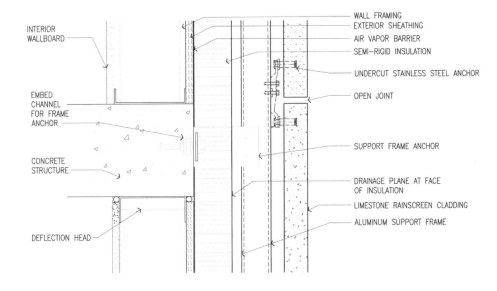

INTERIOR
WALLBOARD

EMBED
CHANNEL
FOR FRAME
ANCHOR

CONCRETE
STRUCTURE

DEFLECTION HEAD

WALL FRAMING
EXTERIOR SHEATHING
AIR VAPOR BARRIER
SEMI-RIGID INSULATION

UNDERCUT STAINLESS STEEL ANCHOR

OPEN JOINT

SUPPORT FRAME ANCHOR

DRAINAGE PLANE AT FACE
OF INSULATION
LIMESTONE RAINSCREEN CLADDING
ALUMINUM SUPPORT FRAME

◀ *Example of a rain screen section detail. The limestone rain screen cladding is anchored to an aluminum frame, which is in turn anchored to semirigid insulation over exterior sheathing. Goody Clancy.*

A rain-screen system is a form of double-wall construction in which the outer layer is panelized with joints that allow air to pass in and out of a cavity while the inner layer is watertight and thermally insulated. Because the exterior cladding is not completely sealed, it is possible for the free movement of air to equalize the pressure between the external atmosphere and the airspace within the wall. This prevents water from being sucked into the air space because of a difference in pressure. Any water that does get in by wind or gravity will run down the back of the outer layer and eventually leave the cavity through evaporation or drainage. The backup wall should be water- and air-tight to prevent the moisture from entering the building.

Exterior insulation and finish systems (EIFS) are waterproof, insulated, finished surface systems. A typical system comprises four layers applied over exterior sheathing: (from inside to outside) rigid polystyrene foam insulation, a fiberglass-reinforcing mesh, a polymer base coat, and a polymer finish coat. This cladding resembles stucco and is sometimes called synthetic stucco. It is inexpensive and versatile, but has limited capacity to withstand impacts, and it does not breathe—any moisture that finds its way behind the cladding will not evaporate well and can damage the building. Drainable EIFS systems, which incorporate drainage grooves and tracks, have been developed to address drainage concerns. Also, EIFS can be modified to work as a rain screen. As with traditional stucco, EIFS is more commonly used in moderate climates.

Any consideration of the building envelope's insulating ability requires an examination of the glazing system. Several tactics can be employed to improve the insulative value of glazing. Windows can be double- or even triple-glazed, and the glass can be treated with a tint or a reflective- or low-emittance coating. The space between the panes of glass can be filled with an inert gas to further improve the assembly's resistance to heat transfer. The choice of frame is significant, as aluminum has a higher thermal conductivity than wood, which in turn has a higher thermal conductivity than insulated vinyl or fiberglass. The structure of thermally broken aluminum windows—which have a spacer between exterior and exterior components to interrupt the thermal bridge—makes them more efficient.

As a general note on envelope insulation, placing continuous insulation on the exterior of a wall assembly typically results in a higher R-value (i.e., resistance to heat transfer) than placing it closer to the interior between framing members, because continuous exterior insulation eliminates thermal bridging at the framing members.

Green Roofs

It is possible to make almost any flat or low-sloping roof a *green roof* (vegetated roof) by providing adequate waterproofing systems, root barriers, and the structural support needed to accommodate the increased weight of a layer of soil or growing medium. Green roofs can be either *intensive* (meaning that they are essentially roof gardens and can have up to several feet of soil and shrubs or trees) or *extensive* (meaning that they include a few inches of growth media and hearty plants like sedum, which require little attention). Key advantages of green roofs are that they minimize storm-water runoff and reduce the heat-island effect (the tendency of certain surfaces to absorb heat, raise the temperature of the surrounding microclimate, and disrupt local ecosystems). They can also be used as terraces to provide an amenity for building occupants or, even when not accessible, to improve the views

of those overlooking the area. There are both built-in-place and modular green roof systems.

Integration of Parking Structures

If a building contains parking, whether at or below grade, the spacing of the columns should be coordinated between the parking and the dwelling unit plans above the garage:

- Columns spaced on 18- to 20-ft centers allow two cars to be parked in between them, and this spacing also provides enough width in the housing unit above for two rooms side by side.
- Alternatively, columns on 27- to 30-ft centers will allow for three cars to be parked between each two columns.

In the other dimension, a single row of parked cars (about 18 ft) with two-way drive behind it (about 24 ft) yields a total depth of about 42 ft. Combined with a width of 20–30 ft between columns, this provides a number of feasible options for the dwelling units above. For example, a townhouse plan above could have 840–1,260 sq ft per floor and be well laid out (see Chapter 4, "The Row House and Other Low-Rise Housing," for typical floor plans).

Two rows of parked cars with two-way traffic between them produces a total building depth of about 60 ft. This depth, combined with the 20–30 ft structural bay, comfortably accommodates flats on either side of a double-loaded corridor. The resulting floor plan for dwelling units offers good flexibility for units of different sizes (note that one parking bay does not need to correspond to one flat). Examples of double-loaded corridor plans are shown in Chapter 5, "The Mid-Rise."

HEATING, VENTILATING, AND AIR-CONDITIONING

Requirements and solutions for heating, ventilation, and air-conditioning (HVAC) vary according to local climate and conditions. The demand on HVAC systems can be significantly reduced by careful selection of a building's orientation and site to allow for good ventilation and shading (in warm climates) or to protect the building from wind and maximize solar gain (in cool climates). Careful design of the building envelope and selection of building materials can further reduce demand by reducing heat loss and solar gain. HVAC systems are selected to meet the remaining demand as well as recover energy in the most efficient, sustainable, and cost-effective way. How initial costs compare to operating costs, market issues, and ownership vary with each project and enter into the selection of the most appropriate method of heating and cooling.

Selection of HVAC Systems for Different Housing Types

Design of a HVAC system generally requires selection of an energy source (traditionally gas, oil, propane, or electricity), equipment to transfer the energy into conditioned air or water (heat exchanger, boiler, air-conditioner, chiller and cooling tower), selection of a medium for distribution (air or water), and selection of a mechanical system to distribute the heating and cooling throughout the building. A mechanical ventilation system may be combined with, or separate from, the heating and cooling system.

The energy source depends on local availability and the comparative costs of oil, gas, propane, and electricity. In some urban or campus settings, steam may be available

from a private or municipal utility or from a central boiler plant. Propane is used in remote locations where neither gas nor oil is available. Ground-source or geothermal power is becoming increasingly popular as an alternative source of energy for both heating and cooling. Ground-source heat pump systems use wells or piping to transfer or collect heat from the ground and/or groundwater, depending on the space available and site geology (soils, substrate and groundwater). Ground-source systems have a high initial cost, which may be offset by the savings from avoiding the capital and operating cost of boilers, chillers, and cooling towers and by the reduction in mechanical space required within the building.

The medium (steam, conditioned water, air, or electricity) and the distribution equipment and system will vary with the size and type of building. Steam distribution systems are outdated and rarely used within new buildings; if steam is provided as the energy source, the heat is transferred through a heat exchanger to a building hot water distribution system, or it may be used to operate an absorptive chiller. Electrical-resistance heating is inexpensive to install but very expensive to operate in most locations. Most housing uses either a conditioned-water or an air system, or a combination of the two. Each system has its own architectural requirements: for example, central air-conditioning or an air system for heating requires space to run ducts both vertically and horizontally, whereas hot water heating requires less space for distribution pipes but requires radiation units within each room.

In one- or two-family houses and townhouses, adequate ventilation may be provided through the use of windows, with limited ductwork for bathroom and kitchen exhaust.

185

Heating and cooling is most often provided either by air running through ductwork (an air system) or conditioned water running either through baseboard finned-tube, radiant panel units or radiators, or through pipes embedded within the floor construction (a water system). Either approach requires a furnace or boiler within the dwelling unit (assuming individual services are provided for each unit), preferably fired by piped natural gas (if available) or oil.

Air systems can also provide cooling and humidity control. The same ductwork and fan that circulates air heated by the furnace can deliver cool air to the rooms. In single-family housing, the central air-conditioning system is typically a split system with an evaporator and fan inside and an air-cooled condenser located outside the dwelling unit—often in a rear garden or on a roof—that cools the air circulated through the building. Alternatively, air-conditioning can be provided by way of window or through-wall air-conditioners; they have a lower installation cost but are visually intrusive and therefore generally less desirable than central air conditioning.

Townhouses can be more energy-efficient than single-family homes because of the large areas of wall shared by dwelling units and the relatively small area of wall exposed to the exterior. It is generally feasible and preferred for each townhouse unit to have independent, metered mechanical systems controlled and paid for by the occupant; however, shared systems may be more economical to install and operate.

All-air systems might be feasible in some low-rise multifamily housing; however mid- and high-rise buildings are rarely heated and cooled by an all-air system, since verti-

cal duct risers and horizontal distribution ducts take up a considerable amount of space in a building. The amount of air required for ventilation is usually much less than that required for air conditioning, so although ventilation air must be tempered, ventilation ductwork is generally not large enough for heating and cooling. A water distribution system will be more economical, with ductwork limited to exhaust and ventilation systems, or to limited distribution of conditioned air within a unit. It is difficult to individually meter a water system in a large building, although the cost of operating fans and equipment within each apartment is generally separately metered along with other electrical loads for each apartment.

Fresh air to apartments in multifamily housing can be provided by operable windows, although most states now require mechanical ventilation to interior corridors and interior rooms, and mechanical ventilation may be required or desired in mid-rise and high-rise multifamily housing. Kitchen and bathroom exhausts remove air from the dwelling unit, which is replaced by fresh air from the windows or ventilation supply system. In some locations, depending on local codes and on the size and construction of the housing, apartment doors may be required to resist the passage of smoke, and then corridors must receive both supply and exhaust air to avoid drawing smoke from an apartment into the corridor in the event of a fire.

Hot water for a multifamily building is typically produced in a large centrally-located gas-fired boiler or by using a steam-to-hot water heat exchanger. This hot water is then distributed to each apartment. Chilled water can also be produced centrally in an electric centrifugal or gas- or steam-fired absorptive chiller in conjunction with a cooling tower, typically located on the roof. The cooling tower can be water-cooled (generally more energy-efficient but with a higher initial cost) or air-cooled (with a lower initial cost but shorter life and lower energy efficiency). Chilled water can also be generated at a central plant and circulated throughout a series of buildings in a campus setting.

Hot or chilled water is pumped to fan-coil units provided in each apartment, zone, or room. In the fan-coil unit, a small electric fan blows air from the room across a coil containing either hot or chilled water. The water in the coil heats or cools that air, which is then distributed through the room or zone. The fan coils are supplied by either a two- or four-pipe water-distribution system.

In a two-pipe system, hot water is piped to the fan-coil unit during heating season, with one supply and one return pipe. When the heating season ends and the cooling season begins, chilled water is circulated through the same pipes. This means that there is a "changeover" in spring when the building's heating system is shut down and the cooling system is started up; there is a second changeover in the fall from cooling to heating. The disadvantage is that only one system can operate at a time. If there is an unseasonably cold morning in late spring after the system has been changed over to cooling, it is difficult to change the system back to heating mode in time to respond—particularly if cooling is required in the hotter, western side of the building later in the day. Automated control systems can shorten, but not eliminate, the time required for a changeover.

With a four-pipe system, both hot water (with one supply pipe and a second return pipe) and chilled water (with a third supply pipe and a fourth return pipe) can be provided at once. This allows better control of the environment during the changeover seasons, providing cooling to any rooms that may need it because of solar exposure or occupancy while the other rooms require heating. Because it requires twice as many pipes, the first cost of a four-pipe system is considerably higher than a two-pipe system. Operating cost can also be higher, since both the boiler and chiller must operate during shoulder seasons.

Chilled beams, which bring cold water into the room along the ceiling to provide cooling, can be used with or without a fan, and they reduce the amount of floor or wall area required for distribution.

Heat pump systems are an alternative to separate furnaces and air-conditioners or condensers for a range of housing types. These HVAC systems use electricity to transfer heat (rather than generate heat). They can provide both heating and air conditioning. Because heat is transferred and not generated, heat pump systems can offer a very energy-efficient alternative in some climate zones or in combination with ground-source heat pump (geothermal) systems. Each room or zone of rooms has its own dedicated heat pump unit; as a result, building occupants can adjust the thermostat setting of each different space as appropriate to its activity or location.

The most common type of heat pump system is an air-source heat pump, which transfers heat between the interior air system and the outside air. This type of system works well for single-family houses or smaller multifamily complexes and in moderate climates, but it is less efficient in very cold climates, where heat pumps that work in conjunction with ground-source (geothermal) systems make for a better choice. The geothermal systems, which transfer heat from a water loop circulated through the ground and then through a heat exchanger to a building's air or water system. They derive their high efficiency from a reliance on moderate underground temperatures that remain constant throughout the year.

In multifamily housing, a water-to-air heat pump system may be more appropriate. Tempered (not heated or cooled) water is generated by a boiler, chiller or ground source, and circulated throughout the building to heat pumps located within each unit or zone. The heat pump extracts heat from, or adds heat to, the tempered-water loop to provide conditioned air to the apartment or space at the desired temperature. This system provides both the convenience of heating and cooling according to different demands or preferences and the efficiency of transferring heat from one zone or apartment (i.e., sunny side of a building) to another zone or apartment (shaded area of a building).

Another alternative for multifamily units is a standalone packaged terminal air-conditioner (PTAC) or heat pump air-conditioner (HPAC), which transfers heat directly through the exterior wall. These units provide individual control and reduce the cost and space required for ducting and central cooling equipment, but they require multiple openings through the exterior wall.

ENERGY

Improving the energy performance of a building helps both the environment, by lowering demand for energy, and the building owner and occupants, by lowering operating and energy costs. Passive solar design, involving the building's orientation, glazing, and thermal mass, can be used to provide thermal comfort and reduce heating and cooling demand. Using efficient HVAC and electrical systems further reduces the energy required to meet the remaining loads. Finally, there are a number of sustainable ways to recover or generate energy on-site.

Building automation systems provide opportunities to improve energy efficiency by monitoring system operation, identifying inefficient operation or system failures, and adjusting operation to more closely match actual demand.

Heat-recovery systems reduce the energy requirements of a building by decreasing the amount of initial energy needed to provide heating, cooling, or hot water. Heat-recovery ventilators recover heat from exhaust air (usually collected from kitchens and bathrooms) to preheat or precool incoming outdoor air. The exhaust air and supply air do not mix, but they travel through adjacent passages within the ventilator to transfer heat. In climates with very humid air, it is preferable to use an *energy*-recovery ventilator, which can recover latent energy as well as sensible energy from exhaust air.

Gravity film exchange (or GFX) can be used to recover energy from wastewater. Narrow copper piping is coiled around a drain pipe and a heat exchange occurs as the warm wastewater in the drain pipe preheats cool water in the copper coil. GFX is ideally suited for instances when the warm wastewater and the need for preheated supply water occur at the same time—for example, during a shower. This is because GFX cannot store heat energy for later use.

Microturbines are small-scale cogeneration turbines that use gas to generate both heat and electricity. Microturbines are most economical when both the heat and electricity that they produce are fully needed and used and where gas costs are low compared to the cost of electricity and other heat sources. Some advantages of microturbine systems over typical generators are the higher ratio of power produced in respect to their size and weight, their low emissions, and the fact that many can be operated without oil, coolants, or other hazardous materials. They can run on renewable fuels like biodiesel and biogas as well as on traditional fuels like natural gas.

Photovoltaic (PV) panels produce direct-current electricity from sunlight. They can be mounted on the roof or walls of a building and are often an integral part of the design. However, the panels' high capital cost means they are often not cost-effective without a subsidy or rebate program. Solar water-heating systems use solar collectors that absorb the sun's heating energy to heat water; they can be cost-effective where there is both consistent sunlight and high demand for hot water.

Mounting individual wind turbines on a building roof is generally not feasible due to cost, vibration, and wind turbulence; however, a range of new products that target both single-family and multifamily markets is becoming available, and municipalities are responding with guidelines and regulations to control their size and use.

Net-zero-energy buildings are gaining considerable interest as a means to reduce energy consumption and reduce greenhouse gas emissions. A net-zero-energy building produces as much energy as it uses over the course of a year. This is possible in

◀ An example of a gravity film exchanger (GFX). The copper coil around the upper part of the drain pipe absorbs heat from departing warm wastewater to preheat incoming cool supply water. Photo by Goody Clancy.

part because the building is very energy-efficient, so its energy requirements are typically 50-70 percent less than those of a comparable structure with no energy-efficient features. Remaining energy needs are usually met through the production of renewable energy on-site. This choice requires commitment from homeowners who are interested in maintaining a sustainable lifestyle. Also, the embodied energy in developing multiple standalone systems must be considered.

PLUMBING SYSTEMS

Plumbing systems typically include domestic hot and cold water, sanitary drain systems, and, for larger buildings, interior roof (storm) drain systems. Gas-distribution piping within a building (for gas-fired heating equipment, hot water heaters, stoves, or dryers) is also considered a part of the plumbing system. In urban and suburban areas, water supply and storm and sanitary (sewage disposal) lines are usually provided by connections to city services. In rural areas without such services, a house or housing complex will need its own well and septic system (which requires substantial open space for a leaching field).

In flat-roofed buildings, rainwater is piped from roof drains through interior drain lines to the storm sewer lines. In new construction, sanitary sewer and storm lines are kept separate both within the building and on-site. This is done because, during storms, the volume of combined sanitary and storm water may be so great that it overwhelms the capacity of sewage treatment plants. Many municipalities require newly constructed buildings to manage storm-water runoff on site, both from the building itself and from impervious parts of the site. Possible strategies for managing storm water on-site include retention systems (such as pervious paving materials, retention ponds, bioswales, and green roofs), which hold the water on-site, and detention systems, which detain or slow the release of water into the municipal systems. Water can also be collected and stored in tanks for discharge back into the groundwater, slow release into a storm-drainage system, or for use in irrigation.

Plumbing within buildings—for kitchens, bathrooms, and laundry—is most efficient if these rooms back up to shared vertical plumbing lines. However, grouping plumbing fixtures horizontally matters less than stacking one bathroom or kitchen over the other, since vertical chases for supply, waste, and vent lines must run from basement to roof.

Hot and cold domestic water supply to fixtures is typically through copper pipe, although cross-linked polyethylene (PEX), is becoming more widely used. Drains from plumbing fixture and vents for those drains are typically cast iron, ductile iron, or polyvinyl chloride (PVC) plastic pipes. These drains typically are collected into a single larger line and exit the building from the basement or below the first floor slab to the sanitary sewer system.

Domestic hot water can be provided from central gas-fired water heaters, from decentralized in-line "demand" heaters, or from a central heating plant in multifamily buildings, with the water distributed to each unit. In multifamily units with a central hot-water source, a recirculating system maintains hot water close to each fixture throughout the system. In-line demand water heaters (also called tankless or instantaneous water heaters) use either a gas burner or an electric element to heat water where and as it is needed, without using a storage tank. These water heaters can be more efficient, because they eliminate both the initial and operating costs of recirculation systems and the heat losses associated with distribution piping and storage; however, demand water heaters do have a limited output capacity.

Water Conservation

As a result of population growth and global climate change, water quality and scarcity have become an issue in many regions around the world, such as the American West. This emerging constraint has increased the need to consider methods of water conservation in housing projects. One tactic is to specify low-flow faucets and showers, dual-flush toilets, and water-efficient dishwashers and washing machines, as well as efficient irrigation systems and programmed irrigation control systems and schedules.

Collection of cooling coil condensate is another way to conserve water. Moisture from the air condenses on the cold evaporator coils of building cooling systems. Usually, drains carry this water into the storm line, but it can also be captured and used. In large buildings, enough water can be produced to supply all of the landscape irrigation needs or a significant portion of makeup water for cooling towers. The most condensate is produced in hot, humid climates like Texas, where the San Antonio library collects 1,400 gallons a day, and in cities where high humidity coincides with annual temperature peaks—for example, Washington, Philadelphia, New York, and Chicago.

Cooling tower blowdown is the process by which water is removed from a cooling tower cycle because the overall concentration of dissolved solids is too high. This water is typically drained to the storm line, but it can be used as graywater. It will usually require some treatment, because of its high mineral content.

Using potable water for toilet-flushing and irrigation no longer has to be the standard. Graywater is wastewater that is collected from showers, bathtubs, lavatories, and clothes washers, as well as certain processes like cooling tower blowdown (but not toilets, kitchen sinks, or dishwashers). Because it is collected with separate drain lines, the building must have a dual-plumbing system. A filtration system removes large particles, and the water is stored until needed for flushing or landscape irrigation. Local codes vary regarding the treatment and allowable use of condensate, storm water, and graywater.

FIRE PROTECTION SYSTEMS

Fire Suppression

Sprinkler systems (i.e., fire-suppression systems) significantly increase life safety and reduce the damage from catastrophic fires in all types of housing construction. They are generally not required for single-family houses, townhouses or low-rise buildings up to three stories in height. Codes or other construction requirements often require sprinkler systems for buildings four stories or taller. The system typically consists of standpipes, connected to horizontal distribution lines at each floor, leading to individual sprinkler heads in each room. Standpipes are vertical pipe risers that are accessible to firefighters at each floor in buildings and allow them to connect their hoses and fight fires floor by floor. Distribution lines must be designed to provide adequate coverage; that is, there must be a sufficient number of sprinkler heads in each room, closet, or other enclosed space to suppress fire. Codes define the number and distribution of sprinkler heads. In the most commonly used "wet pipe" systems (where sprinkler lines are full of water under pressure) individual sprinkler heads are activated by heat rise.

If water pressure in the water line in the street is too low to provide sufficient flow to all floors, or in buildings classified by code as high-rise construction, booster pumps are required to provide adequate water pressure.

Fire Alarm Systems

Local codes (as well as common sense) require, at a minimum, smoke detectors to alert inhabitants to fire. In larger buildings, a more extensive fire-alarm system could include smoke detectors, heat detectors, separate visual and auditory alarms, programmable controls, elevator recall, and a wireless or telephone connection to the municipal fire department.

ELECTRICAL SYSTEMS

The elements of an electrical system generally include:

- A transformer to reduce the line voltage provided by the utility company to the voltage used for distribution within the building (typically 240 V)
- A meter for each building or each unit in multifamily housing, usually at an outside wall where it can be read by the utility company
- A circuit breaker panel within each dwelling unit
- Wiring to distribute electricity to each room and device plate
- Low-voltage systems (to power cable television, computer connections, security system, etc.)

Transformers

In multifamily housing developments, an electrical transformer for every cluster of units will typically be required to step power down from the delivery voltage to residential voltage. The transformer may vary in size from approximately 10 cu ft to several hundred, depending on the number of dwelling units it serves. In its smaller form and on most suburban sites, a transformer may be located outside on the site surrounded by walls, masked by planting, or in a fireproof structure attached to the buildings. In urban areas, it may have to be in a vault under the sidewalk or within the building. Wherever it is located, it must be protected against fire and for electrical safety and meet local requirements for clearances and service access.

Wiring

Electrical wires, (which building codes may require to run within metal conduit for safety) are easily concealed in stud walls but more difficult to deal with in concrete or other solid walls and flooring systems. Running wires to ceiling-mounted lighting in the center of a room looks unsightly with an exposed concrete-plank ceiling, but sometimes the wires can be run in the plank-core holes, or they can be hidden by adding a finished ceiling below the structure. Conduit can be buried in concrete or concrete masonry unit walls and concrete slabs or topping.

Low-Voltage Systems

Low-voltage systems can include cable television; computer and high-speed internet connections; security systems; home theaters and other sound systems; automatic light control; door intercoms and cameras; entry, fire, and temperature sensor systems; telephones; and even central control of window shades.

"Smart homes" incorporate sensors and programmable electronic controls to monitor and regulate indoor environmental conditions and to operate equipment and appliances, typically in an energy-conserving and climatically responsible manner, and often from a remote location. Smart home design can create intelligent environments. For example, sensors in the home can monitor indoor air quality, humidity, and other criteria and then adjust ventilation systems accordingly to circulate fresh air as needed. Sensors can also monitor indoor temperatures and raise or lower blinds to assist with passive thermal regulation. One of the most common features of smart home technology is remote home monitoring for security purposes, allowing a resident to watch his or her house online or monitor whether doors or windows are opened. There are also systems for home automation that make it possible to control the HVAC system or water the lawn from a remote location via the Internet.

SECURITY

Feeling secure in one's home is a basic requirement for well-being. There are both passive and active means of providing security. Passive security measures rely on good planning. Criminal or dangerous activity tends to take place in areas that are not visible from dwelling units or by passersby. Residents should be able to see and monitor the outdoor spaces around their units. Spaces adjacent to units should be clearly private and belong to those units. This both encourages residents to take ownership of them (either literally or symbolically) and

discourages any undesirable activities there. Distinguishing private spaces from public spaces—streets and sidewalks—leaves no unclaimed space that is therefore unwatched, uncared for, and potentially unsafe.

Within buildings the same principles of designing for passive security apply: (1) establishing ownership of spaces and (2) organizing spaces so that they are observed. Minimizing the number of shared entries off a stair or corridor means that residents sharing that space are more likely to know one another and to recognize strangers. Townhouses, with individual entrances to each unit and stairs internal to the unit, reduce public space within buildings to a minimum.

In addition to passive planning measures, active security measures—such as entry alarms; cameras to monitor corridors, entries, or parking areas; and door intercoms with remote releases and other equipment—increase residents' sense that their community is safe. Systems that rely on significant numbers of staff are expensive and can usually be justified only by a large number of dwelling units or expensive housing.

LIGHTING

Within individual dwelling units, a wide variety of lighting strategies are possible, depending on the level of luxury desired. At a minimum, each space will have a switched outlet to allow installation of the resident's freestanding lamps. All public areas will require lights for safety and convenience. Fluorescent lighting is more economical to operate than incandescent and is often used in public areas. Compact fluorescent lighting is also appropriate for residential use and is now available in shapes and warmer tones comparable to incandescent lighting.

Window placement can increase the amount of natural light received by the interior of a building, and decrease the demand for electric lighting. Strategically placed light shelves can help decrease direct glare and reflect light where it is needed. Skylights and solar light tubes are another strategy for bringing natural daylight into a building and reducing the need for electric lighting during the day. Solar tubes have a highly reflective interior coating; they pass through the roof and can bend light up to 90 degrees. Other strategies for reducing energy used for lighting include using dimmers, occupancy sensors, daylight sensors, and energy-efficient light bulbs.

Exterior lighting should provide sufficient light for safety at the point of entry and exit—such as an overhead porch light or a wall-mounted fixture near the door. Lighting the path from the sidewalk or parking area to the door is critical for safety. Lights mounted on poles or high on the building and triggered by motion on the site can contribute to security and safety; however, care must be taken to control the spill of light into apartment windows.

Decorative lighting on surrounding grounds can enhance the view from inside at night as well as provide security. Lighting should be coordinated with landscape design to enhance the use of patios and gardens after dark. It is generally less expensive to light from the walls of the house than to run conduit to fixtures at a distance from the house, but both may be necessary with a large site.

Outdoor lighting should be designed to prevent light from spilling upward toward the night sky to minimize energy use and reduce light pollution.

ELEVATORS

Elevators are not generally provided in single-family or townhouse construction. These housing types assume walk-up access. Because elevators are expensive and their cost must be spread among a large number of units, they are only provided in smaller buildings to serve elderly populations, if required by code for people with disabilities, and in some luxury developments. Small pneumatic vacuum elevators, which do not require an elevator shaft or control room, can be purchased for private units. They fit one or two people and use air pumps to create a difference in air pressure that causes a cab to ascend or descend.

Two major kinds of elevator have traditionally been used in housing: hydraulic and traction (geared or gearless). Hydraulic elevators are used primarily for low- and mid-rise buildings up to six stories. The cab in a conventional hydraulic elevator is moved up and down by a hydraulic piston that requires a hole below the elevator shaft whose depth equals the height of the shaft. Oil is generally used as the driving medium in hydraulic elevators. "Holeless" hydraulic elevators, which have telescoping pistons below or adjacent to the cab, have come into increasing use.

Traction elevators are faster than hydraulic systems, which is an important advantage for taller buildings. They can serve buildings of unlimited height, but they are generally more expensive than hydraulic elevators. Traction elevators operate on a system of counterweighted cables, with the elevator cab raised and lowered by equipment located in a machine room at the top of the shaft. Traction elevators are operated by either geared or gearless systems, the latter being more efficient and more expensive but requiring less maintenance.

A third kind of elevator has been gaining ground in the United States as an energy-efficient and space-saving alternative to traditional technologies. These new elevators are called machine roomless (or MRL) elevators. Developments in technology have enabled a reduction in the size of electric motors used with traction systems, so that the motor can be mounted within the hoistway itself, eliminating the need to have a machine room. MRL systems reduce energy consumption by up to one-half compared to conventional traction systems, and they free up more interior space for programmatic use. MRLs have been slow to catch on in the United States because of required changes in national and local building codes, but their numbers are on the rise.

A review of building height, floor-to-floor height, budget, number of occupants, and expectations on waiting time establishes the needed number, capacity, and speed of elevators. In most large residential buildings, at least two elevators are provided, so that service is maintained if one breaks down. For apartment buildings, the rule of thumb is a 50- to 70-second interval (or longest waiting time) and a handling capacity (or percentage of the building population that can be served by the elevators in five minutes) of 7–9 percent. In many residential buildings, there is no separate freight elevator; a passenger cab is fitted with padding to prevent damage during moving of furniture and deliveries.

At least one elevator cab in a residential building must be large enough to accommodate a stretcher. Size and signal systems of all new elevators must meet handicapped-accessibility requirements. In some cases, especially in existing buildings, a lift may be required to make level changes of up to one story if a ramp is not feasible for wheelchair access. These lifts can move vertically or follow a stair parallel to the rail. Lifts are not always allowed by code and may require a variance.

ACOUSTICS

Noise transmission between units is often a major problem in multifamily housing. Whenever different households live next to or above or below each other in the same building, care must be taken to provide adequate acoustical separation. Some acoustical measures involve planning units so that, for example, a noisy space in one unit is not above or next to a quiet space in the next unit. Other sound-control measures involve the selection and design of building materials and systems. Care must be taken with mechanical systems as well to avoid excessive equipment noise or sound transmission through ductwork.

Noise can be transmitted either by air or through the structure of a building. The ability of a wall or system to reduce airborne sound transmission is measured in sound transmission class (STC) units. The higher the STC rating, the greater the resistance to airborne sound transmission. Particular attention needs to be paid to walls between units and between units and public corridors. Walls between dwelling units should have an STC rating of 52–55. A different standard, impact insulation class (IIC), measures the transmission of structure-borne sound, primarily through the floor system. The IIC rating should be equal to or greater than the required STC rating to provide adequate acoustical isolation of housing units in multifamily housing.

Concrete block walls, with their substantial mass, provide good resistance to airborne sound transmission. Stud walls, used in wood-frame construction, or for partitions in steel or concrete buildings, are inherently lightweight. To increase their mass and resistance to sound transmission, additional layers of gypsum board can be added, typically two layers on each side. The additional mass also works to stop low-frequency transmissions that may not be measured on a standard sound rating test but would be disturbing to building occupants. Resilient channels between the studs and the gypsum wallboard isolate the elements of the wall, reducing structure-borne sound transmission. Fiberglass batt insulation and mineral wool can also be used within walls; mineral wool resists heat transfer better than fiberglass and provides higher STC performance, but it is more expensive. The literature provided by gypsum board manufacturers is a good guide to the STC performance of a variety of wall assemblies. Reduction of airborne sound transmission requires sealing all holes at joints or where building systems penetrate walls and installing gaskets around doors.

The noise of footfalls on a floor, transmitted through the floor structure to the dwelling unit below, is the most common source of noise complaints. As with wall systems, increasing the mass of a floor structure reduces structure-borne sound transmission. A poured-gypsum fill on top of a wood-frame floor increases its mass and reduces sound transmission. Poured-in-place concrete floors, or composite metal-deck and concrete-fill floors, provide good resistance to airborne noise but not to structure-borne (or impact) noise. Carpet and pad absorb some impact and reduce noise transmission

to the floor below. Suspended ceilings also help control impact noise; hanging a gypsum board ceiling on resilient channels further reduces noise by physically separating the ceiling from the floor structure above.

The STC and IIC ratings are based on laboratory tests of wall and floor systems under ideal conditions. Care in both design and workmanship is required to ensure that the finished construction meets the laboratory test level. "Flanking paths," where sound can go around a wall (through ductwork or other openings between units), must be avoided. Elements of the wall or floor structure that are designed to be physically isolated from others must not be inadvertently connected (e.g., by fasteners bridging resilient channels). Any openings that could provide sound paths must be sealed, since a substantial amount of sound is transmitted through small openings.

SUSTAINABLE MATERIALS

The selection of materials is a crucial factor in making a project more sustainable. Materials that are extracted and manufactured locally have a smaller carbon footprint. Many materials can also contain a high recycled content, including steel, concrete, gypsum wallboard, insulation, ceiling tiles, and carpet.

In building interiors, using low-VOC materials and those with no added formaldehyde benefits both the environment and occupants' health. This consideration typically applies to adhesives, sealants, paints, coatings, carpet, composite wood, and agrifiber.

CHAPTER 9
FINANCING AND FEASIBILITY ISSUES

This book has so far focused on the planning and design of housing. This chapter will turn to some key issues in the development process. Although in many ways development is similar for all kinds of projects, certain considerations apply particularly to housing. This discussion is geared to the development of large new projects, but these considerations generally apply equally to adaptive reuse of existing buildings and to small-scale developments.

The development of housing may be initiated by any number of public or private entities: a municipality, a community development corporation, or a nonprofit or for-profit developer. The decision-making process is often defined at the outset or is based on preexisting conditions: for example, a site may be owned by an individual eager to develop it, or a nonprofit organization may have the specific goal of building housing for a particular group and put out a competitive request for proposals to select a developer.

In a conventional development process, the developer hires a planner-architect or sometimes a planner and architect separately. When both planning and architecture are combined in one firm, coordination is simpler and the planning and architectural goals coincide. Occasionally, different firms are hired for the two disciplines—when, for example, a developer admires the designs of an architect whose firm does not provide planning services.

As the project enters successively more detailed planning and design phases, the list of consultants expands to include civil engineers, structural engineers, cost estimators, landscape architects, and mechanical, electrical, and plumbing engineers, as well as other specialists who deal with the legal, marketing, service planning, and property and project management arenas. A construction company may be engaged as a construction manager (CM) at an early stage to perform preconstruction services, which include coordinating budget estimates, arranging for preliminary testing, and advising about construction procedures and practices. For complex projects, the construction manager can help to plan the construction sequence of a project to be built and occupied in phases. Completed plans and specifications may be put out for competitive bid to several contractors or negotiated with one that will to carry out the construction of the project. A CM may act as general contractor and bid various trades to work for them.

The process of developing housing communities—especially for large, multiuse projects—is a complicated, capital-intensive venture not for the faint of heart. It is an iterative process in which development considerations and the physical form influence and change each other at each phase. The developer takes the risk that the project may collapse along the way, but even a project that is proceeding smoothly may change

A rendering can convey a shared vision of a community even before detailed design begins. Goody Clancy.

substantially before it achieves a financially, socially, and aesthetically satisfactory result. We have identified some critical issues or steps in the development of housing. For clarity, we have presented them as though they occur separately and sequentially; in reality they overlap, circle back, and play upon each other.

CONCEPT

At the birth of a project, the developer generally has a vision or goal, which may be established through a market study. He or she may know the demographic of the residents (singles, families, elderly, etc.) and the general character of the housing, including the approximate size of the community; whether the project will be a single housing type, a mixed type, or a mixed-use community; and whether the market suggests renting or selling the units–or a mix of both. The project may be intended to meet some specific profit goals, to take advantage of a specific site, or to conserve a landscape (as in the Prairie Crossing case study in Chapter 3). The successful housing communities shown as case studies in this book are founded on ideals and concepts of community—not profitability alone (although they must be financially feasible to exist). These goals shape decision making throughout the process, although they may evolve over the course of the work to adapt to the practical realities that emerge. For larger projects, the concept may be translated into a master plan that becomes the framework for a development built in phases.

FEASIBILITY PHASE

A critical step in the development process, the feasibility phase establishes the economic, physical, and regulatory feasibility of the project before there is full commitment to proceed. During this phase, the initial concept is shaped and refined. The work of the architect-planner will include:

- A review of all existing information on the site (plot plans, surveys, previous uses, etc.)
- A review of applicable regulations, including zoning and building codes, environmental requirements, and historic regulations (if existing buildings)
- A conceptual site design (or options), locating buildings on the site and including utilities, parking, preliminary roadway, and site amenities
- Counts for parking requirements and number and type of units
- Building-massing studies and unit type preliminary layouts
- Design and construction schedules, including phasing requirements
- Rough cost calculations for budget purposes

During this phase the developer works to estimate costs related to location, size, siting, materials, construction methods, project schedule, and phasing. Just as the physical form of a project affects cost, budget decisions and limitations have an important impact on architecture and planning decisions. Close coordination among the planner, architect, and developer (and all consultants) is critical.

A report--often in the form of a funding, financing, or permitting application—most often presents the result of the intensive research and work undertaken in the feasibility phase, addressing every aspect of the project in a preliminary way. This document creates the framework for further planning and design work (assuming the project is feasible) and communicates this framework to all interested stakeholders on the development team and in the community. The report is the critical vehicle for seeking financing and approvals and probing markets. A careful and thorough feasibility study establishes the credibility and seriousness of a developer and presents a convincing case for the project to a wide audience.

As part of the iterative process of design (as for all architectural projects), each component of the feasibility study will be addressed in more detail in each successive phase: conceptual design, schematic design, design development, and construction documents. The feasibility phase of the process is generally funded by the developer and carried out by all team members, including the architect-planner working with engineers, a construction-cost estimator, and financing, environmental and permitting professionals, among others.

MARKET RESEARCH

Running parallel with the architectural and planning work through the different phases, market research identifies a realistic group of potential inhabitants of a community and defines what will attract them to rent or

▶ *Early site plan showing overall concepts for a project. Goody Clancy.*

Site design concepts

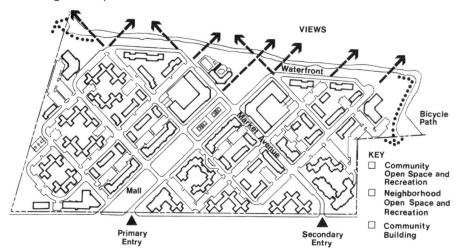

buy. It tests whether the initial concept is a feasible one given the trends in local demographics and economy, community standards, and availability of other housing. If necessary, it guides the developer in reshaping the concept to establish a financially realistic project.

The local and regional economy, employment, family composition, and income all undergo evaluation. The expectations and desires of potential inhabitants are explored, including dwelling-unit size and type and conveniences such as garages, storage, quality of kitchens and baths, security systems, and so on. Shared amenities on the site might include sports facilities, day care and other social services, a concierge, or common social space. Assessing the availability and capacity of local schools becomes important if family housing is planned.

An indispensable tool in this research is the evaluation of other housing projects in the area, both those already completed and those projected (i.e., competitive with the one under consideration). Failing and thriving projects alike yield valuable lessons about vacancy rates, rate of absorption of new units, amenities offered, and selling or rental prices. Estimates of future economic and employment trends (based on educated predictions) inform decisions as well.

Market research may point to the need for a specific kind of housing, known as a niche housing, that is underserved, such as elderly housing or luxury housing for singles, and this, too, may suggest a good opportunity for the developer.

SITE ANALYSIS AND SELECTION

If a project is not tied to a specific site, a suitable site must be selected. The site must be appropriate to the development concept, and the costs of developing that site must be understood at the onset of the project. The

Mix of units across site

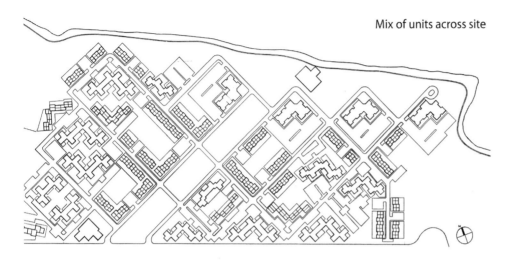

◀ *Drawings show increasingly detailed information about dwelling unit numbers and types and architectural form as the concept develops. Goody Clancy.*

Variety of building types and forms

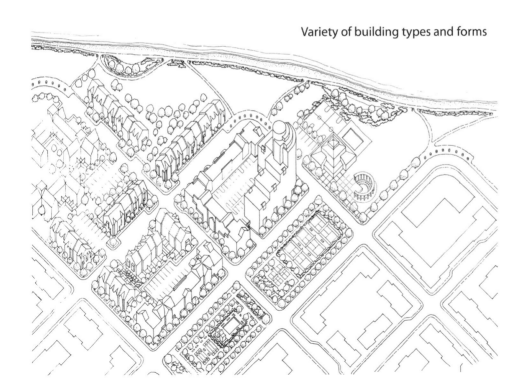

planner-architect or landscape architect may actually do quick, conceptual master plans for more than one site to look at combinations of unit sizes and building types and how all the elements would come together on a given site. She/he looks at how many housing units of what sizes can be accommodated in what building types, how amenities might be located on the site, and how the building forms may be massed on the site.

The process may be complicated and lengthened by the need to assemble several parcels of land to create the site or to demolish existing buildings on the site. An analysis of a proposed (or alternative) site's suitability for housing should address location, infrastructure, environmental issues, construction considerations, and parking. Many of these factors require research and investigation on-site and in public records. A study of all the environmental and social impacts that a construction project would have on the area, known as an environmental assessment (EA), may be required to determine whether there is a need for a more detailed environmental impact statement (EIS). Many projects using federal funding require an EA or EIS before funds are authorized, and many states require such reports be submitted to local governments before a project can be approved.

Location

Views from the site, the availability of public transit, convenience to shops if not provided on-site, and access to employment centers all influence decisions about a site. Compatible conditions and uses surrounding the site are also important in creating a livable community. The identity of abutters to a site and their elected representatives and past history of response to development initiatives is an intangible but critical element in assessing each potential site.

Infrastructure

Based on preliminary calculations of requirements, civil engineers research the availability of adequate roadways and public utilities on or near the a site; the absence of nearby services raises the cost of development. Usually, communities and utility companies charge developers for utility connections. Part of the planning process entails a conceptual approach to distributing utilities such as electricity, sewers, water, stormwater drainage, and gas on the site that conforms to local regulatory requirements, as well as some decisions about a heating or cooling source.

Environmental Issues and Construction Conditions

The site may have built-in constraints that limit the areas that can be built on or that increase the cost of construction. These constraints may be regulatory (e.g., wetlands protected from development), physical (e.g., a high water table or soil types that increase the complexity and cost of construction), or a combination (e.g., the presence of hazardous waste that requires disposal or floodplains that restrict the use of the site). Research into the site issues and testing at this early stage of the project are essential to minimizing unpleasant surprises or even financial disaster later in the project.

Parking

Although parking is but one site consideration, cars often consume a large portion of the site and budget for housing complexes. How parking is handled makes a great difference in determining whether a project becomes a successful community and an attractive place to live. As with many considerations in the planning and design of a housing development, determining how many parking spaces to provide is a complicated issue that involves zoning requirements, location (the project's proximity to jobs, shopping, schools, etc.), access to public transportation, size of dwelling units, whether units are ownership or rental, income of anticipated occupants, and availability of on-street parking. Exploring alternative scenarios for structured and on-grade parking from both design and cost perspectives at this early phase can help a developer avoid a site plan dominated by a sea of cars.

REGULATORY REQUIREMENTS

Municipal, state, and federal regulations all affect housing. Developers must become familiar with the range of regulations, from the Americans with Disabilities Act to local zoning and building codes to the requirements of a historic district. For subsidized housing, there is an additional overlay of occupant income restrictions, locational requirements, design standards, and resident-selection criteria that must be integrated into the normal regulatory structure.

Local zoning laws and their attendant regulatory processes shape housing developments and determine their impact on the surrounding community. Zoning laws lay out:

- Maximum allowable height
- Maximum allowable density
- Number of on-site parking spaces required

These three factors in combination determine the character of a housing development. Although they may be specifically defined in local zoning regulations, these rules are often overridden by such factors as special overlay districts, transfer of development rights, and trade-offs for other community benefits. The final decisions on density, building height, building mass, site utilization, and parking may emerge from negotiations between a municipality and the developer. A well-designed project may allay fears and make a community more receptive to greater density.

▲ *The developer and architect-planner will be required to make several presentations to regulatory bodies over the course of a complex project. Photo by Goody Clancy.*

Building codes affect the cost of the project from the outset, especially where they influence choices about construction type, sprinkler requirements, and materials. Although some building codes are still local, most municipalities have adopted the International Building Code (IBC), which provides consistent standards from place to place. Fire-safety considerations (site layout and on-site roadways, fire separation, detection, and suppression) remain intensely local in practical effect, as fire officials routinely override codes with the support of the municipality.

Informal discussions with local authorities and regulating agencies early in the project can clarify code requirements, establish a constructive pattern of communication, and test the waters for possible relief from some code constraints, while gaining local backing for a project.

FINANCING STRATEGY AND SOURCES

Financing a large development project usually involves numerous sources. A developer may provide a significant part of the equity (investment) financing, but other sources of equity and loans are generally required for a large project. Although the developer may hire specialists to help in seeking financing for a project, he/she should have some expertise in this area.

A careful financial analysis of the costs and income of a project forms part of the due diligence or feasibility study required at the very beginning of a project. A series of cash-flow analyses addresses a project's financial requirements up to and during construction and for operation of the project after completion. At this point, possible funding sources may also be explored. The costs of the initial phases of the project are generally paid for by the developer, since the project is not yet fully defined and too high-risk at this point to attract other capital.

When the project reaches a point where the finances look feasible and the developer has come up with some strategies for financing, a funding package is prepared by the developer. This involves a presentation document that lays out the financial analysis in detail, contains renderings of the physical concept, specifies the number of units, size, and other key information, and generally makes a persuasive argument for the future success of the project and the developer's ability to deliver. The options for development financing after this point are many; financing may change over time and vary with the nature of the project under consideration. Government policies will influence the availability of national or local funds to encourage a particular type of housing (e.g., low-income or rehabilitation of historic buildings) at any given time. For example, federal or state governments can award tax credits to a developer for a project that involves historic preservation, energy efficiency, or the creation of affordable housing. The developer can raise capital or equity for the project by selling the credits to investors who can use them to reduce taxes owed on income from any source.

Depending on the source of equity, the most advantageous ownership structure for a project may be direct ownership or any number of more specialized structures, including real estate investment trusts (REITs) and other corporate entities, partnerships, and joint ventures. Short-term loans for all projects (through the construction period) and long-term loans for rental properties (once the property is occupied and stabilized) will probably be sought. Sources of debt financing may be commercial or savings banks; federal finance programs (usually administered by the Department of Housing and Urban Development or the Federal Housing Administration); tax-credit financing; or credit or insurance companies. Often each lender has specific requirements that influence the project and the process, from planning and design standards to property management and cost guidelines to precompletion sales targets at each stage of funding. A detailed and useful discussion of financial analysis and funding can be found in the Urban Land Institute's *Multifamily Housing Development Handbook* (Schmitz et al., 2000).

COMMUNITY PARTICIPATION

Local regulations may mandate that a developer work with the people who will be affected by a new housing project, but it is generally advisable to start earlier and to carry the process further than required. Direct communication with surrounding neighbors goes far toward allaying fears, dispelling rumors, and starting off on the right foot with a community. When neighbors feel invested in the process and confident that their concerns are being addressed, the development process goes more smoothly. In addition, if community members represent potential inhabitants of the proposed housing, much can be learned by discussing their preferences and concerns. In fact, the process of

◀ *Informal discussion with a community group during the design process. Photo by Goody Clancy.*

discovering and responding to the needs of a group may actually share many features with the marketing campaign.

MARKETING THE PROJECT

Marketing professionals often play a role throughout the development process. They may have input into many aspects of the project planning and design, making sure that the project incorporates locally desirable features and character. The marketing function becomes critically important as

▶ *Further on in the process, a project model helps stakeholders to understand a project. It may also serve as an important marketing tool (along with renderings and model units) to attract sellers or renters before a project is completed. Photo by Goody Clancy.*

selling or leasing begins, usually before completion of construction. The marketer is responsible for establishing model units, creating an advertising campaign, and finding other incentives to attract prospective buyers or renters. Because people ultimately make a community a desirable place to live, marketing that leads to many early sales or rentals can start a beneficial cycle of attracting residents.

BIBLIOGRAPHY

Americans with Disabilities Act. 1999. *ADA Guidelines / Documents and the Fair Housing Act 1999.* Hauppauge, New York: Atlas Publishing.

Benjamin, Asher. 1969. *The American Builder's Companion, or a System of Architecture Particularly Adapted to the Present Style of Building: A Reprint of the Sixth (1827) Edition with 70 Plates.* New York: Dover Publications, Inc.

Binney, Marcus. 1998. *Townhouses—Urban Houses from 1200 to the Present Day.* New York: Whitney Library of Design.

Brown, Lance J., David Dixon, and Oliver Gilham. 2008. *Urban Design for an Urban Century.* Hoboken, NJ: John Wiley & Sons.

Ching, Francis D. K., and Steven R. Winkel. 2000. *Building Codes Illustrated: A Guide to Understanding the 2000 International Building Code.* New York: John Wiley & Sons, Inc.

Congress for the New Urbanism and Michael Leccese and Kathleen McCormick, eds. 2000. *Charter of the New Urbanism.* New York: McGraw-Hill.

Davis, Sam. 1995. *The Architecture of Affordable Housing.* Berkeley and Los Angeles: University of California Press.

Dixon, John Morris, FAIA, ed. 1999. *Urban Spaces.* New York: Visual Reference Publication, Inc.

Dobkin, Irma L., and Mary Jo Peterson. 1999. *Universal Interiors by Design: Gracious Spaces.* New York: McGraw-Hill.

Fader, Stephen. 2000. *Density by Design—New Directions in Residential Development* (2nd ed.). Washington, DC: Urban Land Institute.

Gause, Jo Allen, ed. 2002. *Great Planned Communities.* Washington, DC: Urban Land Institute.

Gauzin-Müller, Dominique. 2002. *Sustainable Architecture and Urbanism: Concepts, Technologies, Examples.* Basel, Switzerland, and Boston: Birkhäuser.

Hunter, Christine. 1999. *Ranches, Rowhouses, and Railroad Flats: American Homes: How They Shape Our Landscapes and Neighborhoods.* New York and London: W. W. Norton.

Jacobs, Jane. 1961. *The Death and Life of Great American Cities.* New York: Random House.

Jones, Tom, William Pettus, and Michael Pyatok. 1998. *Good Neighbors: Affordable Family Housing* (2nd ed.). New York: McGraw-Hill.

Langdon, Philip. 1994. *A Better Place to Live: Reshaping the American Suburb.* Amherst: University of Massachusetts Press.

Mehta, Medan, Diane Armpriest, and Walter Scarborough. 2007. *Building Construction: Principles, Materials, and Systems.* New York: Prentice Hall.

National Association of Home Builders (NAHB). 2006. "Characteristics of New Single Family Homes." Washington, DC: NAHB.

BIBLIOGRAPHY

Newman, Oscar. 1973. *Defensible Space: Crime Prevention Through Urban Design.* New York: Collier Books.

Patterson, Terry. 2003. *Illustrated 2003 Building Code Handbook.* 2nd ed., New York: McGraw-Hill.

Peterson, Mary Jo. 1998. *Universal Kitchen and Bathroom Planning: Design that Adapts to People.* New York: McGraw-Hill.

Plunz, Richard. 1990. *A History of Housing in New York City.* New York: Columbia University Press.

Roessner, Jane. 2000. *A Decent Place to Live: From Columbia Point to Harbor Point.* Boston: Northeastern University Press.

Rowe, Peter G. 1993. *Modernity and Housing.* Cambridge, MA: MIT Press.

Rubman, Ken. 2000. "Community Guide to Saving Older Schools" (booklet). Washington, DC: National Trust for Historic Preservation.

Schmertz, Mildred, ed. 1981. *Apartments, Townhouses, and Condominiums.* 3rd ed. New York: Architectural Record Book, McGraw-Hill.

Schmitz, Adrienne, et al. 2000. *Multifamily Housing Development Handbook.* ULI Development Handbook Series. Washington, DC: Urban Land Institute (ULI).

Schmitz, Adrienne, et al. 2003. *The New Shape of Suburbia: Trends in Residential Development.* Washington, DC: Urban Land Institute.

Shopsin, William C. 1986. *Restoring Old Buildings for Contemporary Uses: A Sourcebook for Architects and Planners.* New York: Watson-Guptill Publishing.

Smeallie, Peter H., and Peter H. Smith. 1990. *New Construction for Older Buildings: A Design Sourcebook for Architects and Preservationists.* New York: John Wiley & Sons.

Stein, Benjamin, and John Reynolds. 1999. *Mechanical and Electrical Equipment for Buildings.* New York: John Wiley & Sons.

Suchman, Diane R. 2002, *Developing Successful Infill Housing.* Washington, DC: Urban Land Institute.

U.S. Green Building Council. 2003 *LEED-NC Version 2.1 Reference Guide.* Washington, D.C.: U.S. Green Building Council.

Willenbrock, Jack H., Harvey B. Manbeck, and Michael G. Suchar. 1998. *Residential Building Design and Construction.* Upper Saddle River, NJ: Prentice Hall.

Standards and Codes

Building Officials and Code Administrators (BOCA). 1998. *BOCA National Building Code/1999.* 14th ed. Country Club Hills, IL: Building Officials & Code Administrators International.

International Code Council. 2009. *International Building Code 2009.* Washington, DC: International Code Council.

U. S. Department of Housing and Urban Development. 1997. *Nationally Applicable Recommended Rehabilitation Provisions (NARRP).* Washington, DC: U.S. Department of Housing and Urban Development. Available on the Internet: www.huduser.org/publications/destech/narrp/toc_narrp.html

INDEX

BUILDING TYPE BASICS FOR HOUSING:

1. Program (predesign)
What are the principal programming requirements (space types and areas)?
Any special regulatory or jurisdictional concerns?
13–20, 27–28, 35, 40–41, 57, 72, 122–123

2. Project process and management
What are the key components of the design and construction process?
Who is to be included on the project team?
144, 146, 162, 197–206

3. Unique design concerns
What distinctive design determinants must be met?
Any special circulation requirements?
7–11, 15–20, 22, 26–30, 34–36, 41–42, 47, 49–52, 55–58, 60–64, 73–74, 79–81, 84–85,
94–96, 98–99, 100–02, 105–08, 110–11, 114–15, 122–27, 129–32, 139–40, 145, 147–48,
150, 159–62, 169–70

4. Site planning/parking/landscaping
What considerations determine external access and parking?
Landscaping?
9, 16–17, 21–22, 26–27, 30, 32–36, 39–41, 44–45, 46, 48–49, 52, 54, 59, 60–62, 65, 76–79,
89–90, 92, 97–98, 105–108, 114–115, 116–118, 120–122, 128, 134, 149–150, 157–162, 200–203

5. Codes/ADA
Which building codes and regulations apply, and what are the main applicable provisions?
(Examples: egress; electrical; plumbing; ADA; seismic; asbestos; terrorism and other hazards)
68, 69–70, 75, 96–97, 123, 144–45, 171–74, 186, 190–92, 202, 203–04

6. Energy/environmental challenges
What techniques in service of energy conservation and environmental sustainability
can be employed?
89–93, 172, 202

7. Structure system
What classes of structural systems are appropriate?
89–93, 172, 202

8. Mechanical systems
What are appropriate systems for heating, ventilating, and air–conditioning (HVAC) and plumbing?
Vertical transportation? Fire and smoke protection? What factors affect preliminary selection?
91–92, 146–148, 185–188, 190–192

9. Electrical/communications
What are appropriate systems for electrical service and voice and data communications?
What factors affect preliminary selection?
154, 192–193